Guidelines

7 / PART 3
...nber 2011

Commissioned by **Jeremy Duff**; *edited by* **Lisa Cherrett**

Guidelines © BRF 2011

The Bible Reading Fellowship
15 The Chambers, Vineyard, Abingdon OX14 3FE
Tel: 01865 319700; Fax: 01865 319701
E-mail: enquiries@brf.org.uk; Website: www.brf.org.uk

ISBN 978 1 84101 635 1

Distributed in Australia by Willow Connection, PO Box 288, Brookvale, NSW 2100.
Tel: 02 9948 3957; Fax: 02 9948 8153;
E-mail: info@willowconnection.com.au
Available also from all good Christian bookshops in Australia.
For individual and group subscriptions in Australia:
Mrs Rosemary Morrall, PO Box W35, Wanniassa, ACT 2903.

Distributed in New Zealand by Scripture Union Wholesale, PO Box 760, Wellington
Tel: 04 385 0421; Fax: 04 384 3990; E-mail: suwholesale@clear.net.nz

Publications distributed to more than 60 countries

Acknowledgments
The New Revised Standard Version of the Bible, Anglicized Edition, copyright © 1989, 1995 by the
Division of Christian Education of the National Council of the Churches of Christ in the USA.
Used by permission. All rights reserved.

The Revised Standard Version of the Bible, copyright © 1946, 1952, 1971 by the Division of
Christian Education of the National Council of the Churches of Christ in the USA. Used by
permission. All rights reserved.

The Holy Bible, New International Version, copyright © 1973, 1978, 1984, 1995 by International
Bible Society. Used by permission of Hodder & Stoughton Publishers, a member of the Hachette
Livre UK Group. All rights reserved. 'NIV' is a registered trademark of International Bible Society.
UK trademark number 1448790.

The New Jerusalem Bible, published and copyright © 1985 by Darton, Longman and Todd Ltd and
les Editions du Cerf, and by Doubleday, a division of Bantam Doubleday Dell Publishing Group,
Inc. Used by permission of Darton, Longman and Todd Ltd, and Doubleday, a division of Random
house, Inc.

The Revised English Bible with the Apocrypha copyright © 1989 by Oxford University Press and
Cambridge University Press.

Revised Grail Psalms copyright © 2008, Conception Abbey/The Grail, admin. by GIA Publications,
Inc., www.giamusic.com. All rights reserved.

Printed in Singapore by Craft Print International Ltd

Writers in this issue

Peter Walker is Associate Vice-Principal and Director of Development at Wycliffe Hall, Oxford, where he lectures in New Testament Studies and Biblical Theology. He has a special interest in the historical Jesus. As a qualified tour guide around Israel, he leads student groups on tours every other year.

Henry Wansbrough OSB is a monk at Ampleforth Abbey in Yorkshire. He is Executive Secretary of the International Commission for Producing an English-Language Lectionary (ICPEL) for the Roman Catholic Church, and lectures frequently across the globe.

James Harding is married to Katie and has two young children. He is the Anglican Chaplain to the students of the University of Liverpool and Liverpool John Moores University, and a licensed lay minister. He completed a PhD in 2006 on the use and influence of the book of Revelation, and, as part of his Anglican ordination training, is working towards a second doctorate in practical Christian Ministry at the University of Chester.

Grace Emmerson has had varied pastoral experience in situations ranging from the Canadian Arctic to urban and rural parish life in England. Her university teaching and writing have been chiefly on Old Testament studies and the Hebrew language.

Kate Wharton is priest-in-charge of a church in Everton, north Liverpool, and is also involved with ministry among deaf people in the Liverpool area. Before ordination she was a speech and language therapist, working with children with a variety of communication difficulties. She is and always has been single and counts it a privilege to speak and teach on this important but often neglected topic.

Jeremy Duff is a vicar in Widnes with a teaching and writing ministry, which has included posts at Liverpool Cathedral and within Oxford University. His writings include *Meeting Jesus: Human Responses to a Yearning God* (SPCK, 2006) and *The Elements of New Testament Greek* (CUP, 2005).

Rosie Dymond is Rector of the Parishes of Bedwellty and New Tredegar and is excited about the many signs of God's kingdom in the beautiful post-industrial Valleys of South Wales. She is especially interested in community ministry and the arts. She has an academic background in neuroscience research and previously served as Assistant Chaplain at the Church of St John and St Philip in The Hague.

The BRF Prayer

Almighty God,
you have taught us that your word is a lamp for our
feet and a light for our path. Help us, and all who
prayerfully read your word, to deepen our
fellowship with each other through your love. And
in so doing may we come to know you more fully,
love you more truly, and follow more faithfully in
the steps of your son Jesus Christ, who lives and
reigns with you and the Holy Spirit,
one God for evermore. Amen.

A Prayer for Remembrance

Heavenly Father, we commit ourselves to work in
penitence and faith for reconciliation between the
nations, that all people may, together, live in
freedom, justice and peace. We pray for all who
in bereavement, disability and pain continue to
suffer the consequences of fighting and terror.
We remember with thanksgiving and sorrow those
whose lives, in world wars and conflicts past and
present, have been given and taken away.

FROM AN ORDER OF SERVICE FOR REMEMBRANCE SUNDAY,
CHURCHES TOGETHER IN BRITAIN AND IRELAND 2005

The Editor writes...

Where is God? Many people, at some time in their lives, find themselves asking this question, whether in the quiet darkness of their silent suffering or in an anguished, heartfelt cry. When we look out on a world from which God's love and activity seem absent, it is hard not to doubt whether God himself has departed.

Most of our readings in this edition relate to this sense of God's seeming absence. We begin with the final part of Peter Walker's notes on Matthew. Here we find parables about the bridegroom's absence, followed by Jesus' betrayal, trials and death, culminating in the cry, 'My God, my God, why have you forsaken me?' Then we encounter Psalms 51—63, guided once again by Henry Wansbrough—psalms that express confidence in God even in times of great hardship or challenge.

A new contributor, James Harding, explores Revelation with us, a book which seeks to convince us that even if evil seems to be triumphing around us, God is actually in control. Then, accompanied by Grace Emmerson, we read Habakkuk, a lesser known Old Testament prophet, who speaks out in a violent world in which God seems silent.

After Habakkuk, we turn to something a little different and explore singleness with another new writer, Kate Wharton. Many people in our society and churches are single, whether never married, separated, divorced or widowed. What particular challenges and joys do they experience? What does the Bible have to say about singleness? Next, Jeremy Duff guides us through the book of Daniel. The book is set during the exile, that terrible time when the Jewish people came to terms with the destruction of the temple and their separation from the land, but it seems also to speak into later times, when further calamities overtook Israel.

For Christmas we are in the hands of Rosie Dymond, who brings traditional 'cock-crow lullabies' alongside the biblical accounts of Jesus' birth, to refresh our encounter with the Christmas story. Finally, we read the book of Haggai, again with Grace Emmerson. Here we find the Jewish exiles returned to the land, yet they are struggling and God's temple still lies in ruins. Why have things not turned out as they had hoped?

We hope this edition will help you understand and respond aright to the sense of God's absence, whether now is a painful season in your own life, or whether you need to be equipped to serve the people around you.

Jeremy Duff, Commissioning Editor

Matthew 25—28

We finish our year's study of the second half of Matthew's Gospel with the final four chapters. Previously, Jesus has been urgently challenging his audience of followers and opponents to recognise and acknowledge his identity as Messiah, thinking beyond their limited view of what that title might mean. He has asked them to interpret the 'signs of the times' in his present teaching and ministry; he has asked them to interpret a range of Old Testament imagery from the past. Now, speaking again in parables, he focuses on future judgment and the eternal significance of their response to him.

At last, however, the time for picture language runs out. As Jesus himself blows open the 'messianic secret' (26:64), the 'hour' has come for a decision to be made: is he who he claims to be and what, in the end, must be done about it?

Of course, the story does *not* end there. None of those who believe they are directing events—has the final say: they are not in control. The resurrection reveals Jesus unequivocally as the living God, to be worshipped and obeyed.

1 Watch and wait

Matthew 25:1–13

We resume our readings in Matthew in the final chapter of his fifth discourse (the first one was the Sermon on the Mount: chs. 5—7). This final discourse (chs. 23—25) begins with seven 'woes' and includes some of Jesus' most challenging teaching, as he confronts Jerusalem's leaders and then warns of God's judgment on the city at the time of the 'coming of the Son of Man' (24:27, 30). In my comment on Matthew 24 (last May), I noted that this 'coming', confusingly, refers both to the events of AD70 (when Jerusalem's temple was destroyed) and to Jesus' second coming. In our parable today, both possible meanings need to be borne in mind.

This parable is expressly about how the kingdom of heaven will operate at a surprising, unique moment in the future ('*Then* the kingdom will be like…': v. 1). This is how it will be on that day, Jesus warns. He has already spoken about a 'day' when, after a delay, the Lord will come, surprising his servants at an 'unexpected hour' (24:42, 44, 50). Today's parable is expanding on the same theme: get ready; don't be found doing the wrong thing at the crucial moment; or (in Jesus' one-word punchline: v. 13) 'Watch!'

Without over-applying each element of the parable, there are two main things that stand out. First, those waiting for that day should not be surprised by its delay but are to plan accordingly (the foolish virgins took only a limited supply of oil, with no spares). Jesus' first hearers were not to be surprised that Jerusalem's judgment did not happen immediately (there was a wait of 40 years before AD70); nor are we to be surprised that Jesus' second coming has been delayed. Second, that day (when the bridegroom comes) is to be our most important goal in life. It was not merely 'unfortunate' that the foolish virgins missed the groom's arrival: to accompany him was the precise purpose for which the bride had asked them to be her companions; it was their *raison d'être*. So, too, we should see that day, when our Master Jesus (though currently invisible) is made manifest to all, as our greatest joy. In what ways are we in danger of forgetting this, or of being concerned with other priorities (effectively 'away on other business')? We do not want to hear Jesus say to us, 'I do not know you' (v. 12).

2 A good investment

Matthew 25:14–23

Jesus continues with a similar parable: this time, however, we are waiting not for the arrival of a bridegroom but for the return of a man who in today's world might be termed an investment manager. Jesus' teaching about the 'coming of the Son of Man' (24:36–51) had highlighted the need for two things (staying awake and labouring for the absent master); yesterday's parable picked up the first emphasis ('keep watch!') and today's parable picks up the second ('keep working').

This is an important balance. We are to be appropriately focused on

Jesus' return, but not to the extent that we sit around doing nothing in the meantime. Intriguingly, this may have been the temptation into which some Christians fell in Thessalonica after they had received Paul's teaching about Christ's return (hence Paul's warning against idleness: see 1 Thessalonians 4:11; 5:14; 2 Thessalonians 3:6–14). Jesus' teaching here is even stronger than Paul's, giving us a graphic picture of the way God wants us to be working on his behalf during the apparent absence of our master.

In the parable's first half, the focus is on the two servants who are praised for their investment. We often fail to notice the extravagant generosity of the master: a 'talent' was roughly the equivalent of what a hired labourer would be paid if they worked for 20 years. This means that the two talents—let alone the five—amount to a lifetime's salary! So, even if the end of the parable reveals the severity of the master, the whole story is premised on his kindness (compare, for example, Romans 11:22). God is a generous giver and gives in 'abundance' (v. 29).

What exactly, however, is it that he has given? He has given us our physical, created life: it is a gift. He has given us, in the gospel of Christ, undeserved kindness and forgiveness with the promise of life eternal: all this is pure gift. And, yes, he then gives to his servants further things (financial resources, spiritual gifts, personal talents in another sense), all of which he expects to be used for his kingdom. God is looking for a return on his investment. He wants to find that his 'stake' in the world has increased as a result of our careful deployment of his generous resources. The question is: are we putting our resources towards the building up of God's kingdom or our own?

3 Wasted gifts

Matthew 25:24–30

So far, so good; but this second half of the parable is disturbing. There was 'gnashing of teeth' back in 24:51, but there it was meted out on a drunken, bullying steward: here the recipient was simply timid (v. 25). He did not steal the master's gift but simply gave it back to him untouched. What was so wrong with that?

Jesus' key point is that God is expecting a return on his investment (described as 'reaping' where he had not personally 'sown': vv. 24, 26). The recipient may see this as a sign of the giver's 'hardness' (v. 24) but Jesus is effectively saying, 'Tough! That's how it is. God's gifts come with an insistence that they increase the giver's glory and kingdom.' They are therefore not to be squandered with ingratitude or even 'returned to sender' unopened; rather, they are to be joyfully received as gifts and daringly used to advance God's purposes.

There are salutary warnings here to everyone—not least to those who do not see their own created life as a precious gift from God; who therefore live their lives entirely for their own benefit and who, at their death, effectively give back to God the gift of life with no gratitude to the giver and no intention to have brought him any glory or praise.

Yet, as we saw yesterday, there are warnings here to believers as well—those who acknowledge that they have received their redeemed, spiritual life as a gift from God (not to mention other gifts and resources). Let's not be sullenly indifferent to what we have been given ('wicked': v. 26) or simply too lazy to do anything with it ('slothful': v. 26); rather, we should get out there and put all these gifts to good use.

There are two final points. First, although it is easiest to see the 'man' (25:14) as a reference to God, almost certainly this is Jesus referring to himself (Jesus can easily be identified with the 'bridegroom' and the 'Son of Man' in vv. 1, 31). If so, Jesus himself is the 'hard master' who goes away but returns with high expectations of his servants' activity. Second, there are hints of further gifts after Jesus' return—'many', 'more' and 'abundance' (vv. 21, 23, 28, 29). The nature of these gifts in the new resurrection life is only hinted at elsewhere (see Matthew 25:34) but Jesus' teaching here encourages us to believe that they will be worth waiting for.

4 Responding to Jesus

Matthew 25:31–46

Jesus' long discourse climaxes with the powerful parable of the sheep and goats, which, though frequently quoted, is perhaps one of the most difficult to interpret correctly.

One of the parable's most remarkable features is the sheer glory that

Jesus now unapologetically ascribes to his own identity: he is the 'Son of Man' who will sit on a 'glorious throne'. In this kingdom of heaven, God's own kingdom, he himself is described as the king (vv. 34, 40)—clearly a divine role. He is implicitly also the Son of God, since he tells the sheep on his right that they are 'blessed by my Father' (v. 34). Twice he is described as 'Lord' (vv. 37, 44), and he has been given by God the ultimate role of judging the human race (not just individuals but entire nations: v. 32), sifting them as straightforwardly as a farmer sorts out the sheep from the goats at the end of a hard day's walk. These claims by Jesus are simply staggering—indeed, monstrous and outrageous if not true. Familiarity with this parable, or unresolved discussions over its precise interpretation, should not blind us to the enormity of Jesus' portrait of his own uniqueness and glory.

Once we see this, we can better recognise Jesus' chief point in the parable—that people's eternal destiny truly hangs on their response to him. The key criterion in this judgment is whether people (knowingly or unknowingly) have done things 'for me' (v. 40) or not (v. 45). Jesus is not only the judge but also the yardstick by which he judges.

A positive response to Jesus can be seen, however, not just in an individual's explicit faith in him and obedience to his Lordship but also in charitable acts expressed to his 'brothers and sisters' because they belong to Jesus' family. The parable is expanding on the teaching that Jesus has given in 10:40–42: 'He who receives you receives me... if anyone gives even a cup of cold water to one of these little ones because he is my disciple... he will certainly not lose his reward.'

Jesus is thus teaching again that there is now an invisible but real relationship between himself and his followers, and the way people respond to Jesus' followers could determine their eternal destiny. Thus, although the parable obviously encourages us to be caring towards other human beings who are all made in the image of God, it does not teach that such humanitarian concern is itself an automatic means of salvation—an alternative track by the 'back door' into God's kingdom for secularists who, for whatever reason, cannot believe in his Son. No, Jesus is looking—albeit across a graciously wide sphere of activity—for evidence of a positive response to himself.

5 Anointing for burial

Matthew 26:1–13

Suddenly everything changes. The discourse on the Mount of Olives (24:3—25:46), which climaxed with the Son of Man on his glorious throne (25:31), ends with Jesus reminding his disciples that this same Son of Man will soon be crucified. It's a powerful juxtaposition, which we must keep in mind as we now read through Matthew's passion narrative: despite appearances, the man being led to death is also the king of glory.

Down in the city below (Caiaphas' palace would have been in the 'Upper City' on the western side of Jerusalem), plans are indeed underway to eliminate Jesus. God's good plans and purposes, as revealed through Jesus' prophetic prediction, are thus, strangely, coming to pass through human plots and machinations which are evil. We can sense how this passion narrative is operating at two levels—the human and the divine (see also 26:24).

Jesus remains on the Mount of Olives. If he had been sitting overlooking the city on the western side of the Mount (24:3), then a half hour's walk going eastwards would have brought him to Bethany. This small village, the last outpost of habitation before the Judean desert, was almost certainly Jesus' base of operations during these crucial days (see Luke 21:37). He and his twelve disciples may have stayed in various homes, including those of Lazarus (with Mary and Martha) and perhaps Simon the leper (v. 6)—presumably someone who had been healed of his leprosy and was therefore no longer living in isolation.

The story of Jesus' anointing is recounted also in Mark 14:3–9 and John 12:1–7; John explicitly identifies the woman as Lazarus' sister, Mary. Although Mary was a very common name, this Mary may possibly be identified with Mary Magdalene (who herself may have been the woman who anointed Jesus in a similar way back in Galilee: Luke 7:36–50). Either way, this is the woman who, in contrast to the male disciples, intuitively recognises that Jesus is indeed about to die and offers him a gesture of her love and honour. What ways can we discover to express to Jesus our own love and honour?

The men, looking on, see only its extravagance and financial stupidity. For Jesus, however, who never experienced on the human level either a wedding or a coronation (though he is the ultimate bridegroom and king), this is a poignant moment, which he gratefully receives as an advance anointing for his burial. No wonder Mary was anxious a few days later, after Jesus had died, to perform the same act of love to his corpse (Matthew 28:1); but on that occasion she was denied the opportunity through circumstances beyond her control.

6 Human betrayal

Matthew 26:14–25

Matthew's account will give special prominence to Jesus' being betrayed by Judas Iscariot (26:47–56; 27:3–10). We will never know Judas' precise motivation—though perhaps it was triggered by the event in Bethany, where Judas could sense that Jesus, rather than fighting for his Messiahship, was already resigned to his death. Judas' personal agenda for Jesus was now a lost cause. For the chief priests, who could not think of a way of arresting Jesus discreetly during the busy and crowded week of the Passover celebrations (26:5), Judas' offer of assistance was just what they needed, together with his report that Jesus would seemingly not be offering much resistance.

So Jesus now has a would-be traitor among his own intimate group of followers. The psalmist spoke of the wound inflicted not by the hatred of one's obvious enemies but by the treachery of a friend: 'It is not an enemy who taunts me—then I could bear it... but it is you, my companion, my familiar friend. We used to take sweet counsel together...' (Psalm 55:12–14). Jesus is enduring one of the most painful of human experiences: all the love and trust he has invested in Judas over several years is now being cruelly thrown back in his face. If this is something that you yourself have experienced, you will know its pain; but you can also learn from today's passage that Jesus knows at first hand what you have been through.

Not surprisingly, this painful 'inner' story within the wider passion narrative comes pointedly to the fore in Jesus' last supper with his friends: 'One of you will betray me' (v. 21). You can almost hear the shock go round the room. The other disciples ask innocently (perhaps Jesus knows something about them that they themselves do not yet know!)

but Judas asks knowing that he has a guilty secret—and it shows. Jesus' reply ('You have said so') reveals how he takes Judas' innocent-sounding question as really a statement of malicious intent. It's hard to deceive successfully at such close quarters—and especially when it's Jesus who is looking you straight in the eye. Are there any ways in which we are trying to deceive those closest to us? More pointedly, are we playing games of some kind with the risen Jesus? His eyes are like a 'flame of fire' (Revelation 1:14), so it's hard to hide from his penetrating gaze.

Guidelines

One of the most powerful things to note in our readings this week is the sharp contrast between Jesus' authoritative words recounted in chapter 25 and the start of the passion narrative in chapter 26. The Jesus who begins the slow, solemn road towards his death is precisely the same Jesus who is the exalted Son of Man or king who sits in judgment over humanity 'at that time... when he comes in glory'. It's hard to hold these contrasting perspectives on Jesus together in our minds: how can they both be true of the same person? Yet, as we hold them together, we are taken deeper into the mystery of the cross—that this place of suffering was entered into by one who was an eternal King. The one who was truly 'God with us' went to the place of utter Godlessness and desolation in order that we who were 'without God' might now discover 'God with us' (Matthew 1:23; see also 2 Corinthians 5:21; 8:9). Let's hold this in mind as we follow Jesus to the cross in our readings over the next two weeks.

1 Passover symbolism

Matthew 26:26–29

Passover was the annual springtime festival when the Israelites celebrated God's deliverance of his people from Egypt under Moses—especially the way God's judgment had 'passed over' Israel's firstborn sons because their homes were daubed with the blood of a lamb (Exodus 12:12–13). In

Jesus' day, those who were visiting Jerusalem tried to celebrate the main Passover meal within the city walls (hence the discussion in 26:17–18). There was also a deep longing that God would work a repeat deliverance for his people—this time not from Pharaoh but from the pagan Roman authorities. When would God's kingdom come?

By ensuring that his last meal with them was filled with Passover symbolism, Jesus was effectively saying to the disciples, 'When you look back on this unique weekend, interpret my actions through the lens of Passover: if you're looking for deliverance, for the coming of God's kingdom, for the removal of God's judgment, you will find it all right here—though it may look quite different from what you were expecting.'

We too need to use this lens as we interpret Jesus' death and resurrection (note that the resurrection is hinted at in verse 29 and mentioned explicitly in verse 32). Yes, we may find some of the exodus story quite alien to our ears, but God truly worked this deliverance in history to give us, in advance, the tools with which to interpret his eventual work in Jesus. Through Jesus, God's people are redeemed (brought from slavery into freedom) and rescued from divine judgment, being truly offered 'forgiveness of sins' (v. 28). Do we know that and give thanks for it?

Ever since, one of the best ways to give thanks for God's great redemptive act has been, of course, to 'break bread' in Jesus' name—to repeat what Jesus went through here with his disciples. Jesus was deliberately not just teaching them that they were to see his body as being like the Passover 'bread of affliction' and his blood like the 'cup of redemption'. He was also giving them a meal to celebrate, which would involve all his future followers in the enactment of a dramatic visual aid. Have we joined in this meal recently? The risen Jesus expects 'all' of his followers (v. 27) to 'drink his blood'. To his first disciples as Jews (forbidden by God to drink blood: Leviticus 17:10–12), this symbolism would have seemed horrific, but Jesus knew that his followers could not evade this demanding encounter, this close involvement with the one who alone died to bring them life and forgiveness (John 6:53–54).

2 Cup of judgment and salvation

After the last supper somewhere in Jerusalem's Upper City, Jesus goes down some of the steep steps to the Lower City, out through the Siloam gate, and then northwards up the dark Kidron valley towards a secluded olive grove called Gethsemane. During this 40-minute walk, Jesus' disciples sing some 'hymns' (possibly the Hallel Psalms 113—118) and Peter makes some remarks he will soon regret (see notes on 26:69–75).

Jesus needs some time on his own, but also an element of friendly support (Peter, James and John are to stay nearby). Now the enormity of what Jesus has set his face to accomplish falls upon him like a dead-weight (vv. 37–38). It's one thing to become convinced that you are called to be Isaiah's suffering servant, but quite another now to suffer; you may have calmly predicted your vindication and resurrection (as in 26:32), but the only way to be proved right is to be killed—and the 'hour' for that is now evidently 'at hand' (v. 45). All this requires incredible trust in God and a steely determination to complete the task.

No wonder Jesus prays ('with loud cries and tears' according to Hebrews 5:7), falling prostrate on the ground (v. 39). This is the time when he needs to know the reality of his unique relationship with God, to utter that word '*Abba*' ('my Father': vv. 39, 42) and know deep down that it is profoundly true. Yet, as he listens for the Father's authentic voice (affirming his unique identity as his Son), he also hears that same voice assure him that he has not misheard his unique vocation. Yes, there is a 'cup' and he needs to drink it. There is no other way.

We too might wish there had been some other way for God to forgive human sin. Yet Jesus asked precisely that question and was given a solemn 'No'. Scholars and sinners alike have ever since tried to wriggle round this: could not God forgive without the death of his Son, or without such a bizarre method of 'atonement'? However, if we admire that figure in the garden and claim to be his followers, then we should humble ourselves under this revelation, not arguing with God but being profoundly grateful. After all, if the 'cup' was a symbol for the cup of God's wrath (Isaiah 51:17; Jeremiah 25:15; Ezekiel 23:32–33), Jesus has now—amazingly—drunk that cup of judgment to the dregs. As a result, what is offered to us is a 'cup of salvation' (Psalm 116:13), bringing us God's 'forgiveness' (Matthew 26:28). Perhaps it's we who should be falling down prostrate before our God?

3 Passive power

Matthew 26:47–56

As fishermen, they might have been expected to keep awake at night; yet, in Gethsemane, Peter, James and John fall asleep three times (26:40, 43, 45). This is a clear hint that Judas' arrest party did not arrive till very late—probably after midnight, perhaps even as late as 2 a.m. This highlights two things.

First, when Caiaphas received Judas' tip-off, he was unable to respond immediately because he needed first to consult with Pontius Pilate as to whether he would hold trial the next day and would issue a death sentence. After all, there was no point in risking a riot by having Jesus stuck in prison during the week-long festival of Unleavened Bread (26:5). The fact that Pilate's wife has a bad dream about Jesus that night (27:19) further suggests that Caiaphas visited Pilate's residence for a consultation and Pilate told his wife why he had been disturbed at so late an hour.

Second, it underscores the fact that Jesus could easily have escaped arrest. Another 30 minutes' walk, up over the Mount of Olives, would have brought him back to Bethany (which is where, almost certainly, the disciples fled: v. 56). Instead, Jesus did the hardest thing—waiting. Some (like Judas?) had expected him to fight, storming into Jerusalem; others would now have advocated flight (back to Bethany and the desert beyond). Jesus did neither. He waited—out of his love for you and me.

Once again, this is a strong indication that Jesus deliberately gave himself up, of his own volition—because this was indeed his Father's will (26:39, 42). Thus Jesus twice emphasises that these strange events are happening because they fulfil God's will as revealed in scripture (vv. 54, 56). Jesus' words also reveal his incredible authority: twelve legions of angels are effectively at his beck and call (v. 53), but this power is being deliberately left unused. So Jesus may appear passive and powerless but the deeper reality is that he is truly powerful—and, paradoxically, in active control of what is being done to him. His disciples are rebuked for taking steps to change the situation (v. 52); we too need to bow before this insistence of God—to redeem us through Jesus' death.

Judas now does the evil deed. Instead of hiding behind his henchmen, he himself comes forward and greets Jesus with a kiss. This normal sign of respect to a rabbi (26:25, 49) is now twisted, almost sneeringly, into a cruel act of betrayal and the signal for Jesus' arrest. It's a brutally conscious act. Are there ways, even if far less conscious or significant, in which we are betraying the one we claim to love?

4 Messiah and king

Matthew 26:57–68

Jesus, now a prisoner, is led back into the city, returning via a different route to the Upper City—the quarter inhabited by Jerusalem's wealthier citizens, such as Caiaphas the high priest. Often their houses were built round a small square open to the sky (a 'courtyard': v. 58), with large adjoining rooms. Into this opulent environment, embellished with the latest fashions of wealth and power, some guards usher in an impecunious prophet from rustic Galilee.

Meanwhile, some bleary-eyed men, summoned from their beds, begin to gather as well—members of the Jewish ruling council (the Sanhedrin). In their eyes, this Jesus is a political agitator, something that these Jerusalem aristocrats fear and hate; they would prefer him dead. Yet 25 years earlier they had lost the right to issue a death sentence, so they will need the Roman governor's involvement and must therefore charge him with a political crime. Yet they are also concerned on religious grounds, for he has said and done things to suggest that he may be the Messiah.

In particular, the Messiah was expected to have authority over the temple, 'restoring' it in some sense. Jesus' temple-cleansing had raised the issue of his authority (21:12–13, 23), so that is what they now want to interrogate him about. Two witnesses give a slightly twisted version of a statement that Jesus had indeed made in the temple (v. 61; see the exact version in John 2:19), including a bizarre claim that he could 'restore' or 'rebuild' it in just three days. Matthew's readers can see this as a reference to the resurrection 'on the third day' (16:21; 17:23; 20:19) but Jesus' hearers can only see it as dangerous megalomaniacal nonsense.

So Caiaphas, putting Jesus 'on oath', demands to be told if he is this Messiah. Now, at last, Jesus breaks silence: the 'messianic secret' is out. He is indeed the Messiah (the human king desired by Israel), but—far more outrageous than that—he is also the exalted 'Son of Man' who will soon be vindicated in God's throne room and allowed to sit in the place of supreme power at God's 'right hand' (v. 64; see 1 Timothy 6:13–16). For Caiaphas, this is evidence enough of 'blasphemy'—not because in those few words Jesus has claimed to be eternally 'divine' (as Christians would now, rightly, see it) but because it is outrageous for a human being to present himself as the person given such unique authority by Israel's God (the 'Power'). In so declaring (just a part of) his identity, Jesus has given ample ammunition to the religious leaders. And, fortunately for them, the word 'Messiah' can also be translated 'king' (27:11). That should sound 'political' enough for Pilate.

5 Peter's denial

Matthew 26:69–75

Meanwhile, outside is Peter. This Peter had been the first to blow open the 'messianic secret' and had therefore been renamed by Jesus as the 'rock'. On this rock Jesus would build his church, which then would stand firm against the very 'gates of hell' (16:16–19). But now Peter falters before a couple of servant girls. Inside the palace, Jesus is owning up to his messianic identity; outside, Peter is disowning it. What Peter had been able to assert in private near Caesarea Philippi, he cannot say in a more public setting in Jerusalem.

We know this story well and it's easy for us to be very hard on Peter at this point, implying perhaps that we ourselves might have fared better. Hindsight is a marvellous thing. If Peter had known for a fact that Jesus would be raised again in three days (and also that his failure would be emblazoned throughout the world for the next 2000 years; compare 26:13), he might have acted differently. Above all, if he'd known that the religious authorities were only interested in arresting Jesus—no one else—things might have been different. But he did not know. He believed himself to be in real danger.

In some ways, he had done well to get this far. The other disciples had scarpered up the Mount of Olives (26:56); they had indeed been 'scattered' as soon as the shepherd was attacked, just as Jesus had predicted (v. 31). Peter, perhaps because he wanted just to be different from the rest (v. 33), had sworn complete loyalty to Jesus; so, instead of fleeing, he had bravely tagged along behind the arrest party (with just one other disciple, probably John: see John 18:15–16). Then he succeeded in gaining entrance into the inner courtyard, but what was he going to do next? He was very exposed, standing around in a small crowd of people at this unearthly hour in the morning; and every time he opened his mouth, his Galilean accent betrayed him further (v. 73).

To hear that rooster crow must have been a sickening moment for Peter. He had let Jesus down so badly, and Jesus had known his weakness all along. Yet Jesus not only knew but also had a plan of restoration: once raised from death, Jesus would meet with Peter and all the other disciples (26:32), and that would be the time of restoration and forgiveness (28:16–20; see also John 21).

6 Daybreak

Matthew 27:1–10

With sunrise in springtime at 6 a.m. the rooster would have crowed some time after 4.30. This confirms the likelihood (see above) that Jesus' arrest took place well after midnight. Perhaps he arrived back at Caiaphas' house around 3 a.m. (Peter would then have been in the courtyard for about an hour at the most). This also explains why there seems to have been a 'repeat' meeting of the Sanhedrin (v. 1), for the first interrogations would have been made only by the few council members who were up at this unusual hour. Since, strictly, council meetings were not supposed to be conducted at night, there would inevitably be a proper meeting after daybreak—a quorate gathering for 'all' the elders. This was the official moment when the death penalty was formally ratified.

Daybreak also brings new awareness to Judas. A lot has happened since his interchange with Jesus in 26:25—leaving the disciples at their meal, going to Caiaphas' house, perhaps joining him on a sudden visit to the governor, then leading the arrest party to Gethsemane and presumably standing by as a witness during Jesus' trial. At some point, Judas begins to change his mind. If the 'final straw' was seeing Jesus being handed over to Pilate for execution (v. 3), it's possible that he himself had never wanted Jesus killed. Perhaps he betrayed Jesus presuming the religious authorities would soon discover what he himself had realised—that Jesus offered no real political threat. If so, they would probably simply send him back to Galilee. Now Judas realises how naïve he has been.

Alternatively, maybe something struck Judas about Jesus' utter 'innocence' (v. 4); or perhaps he came to see that Jesus was indeed, even if not the political Messiah for whom he and others had hoped, the exalted Son of Man whom God had truly appointed (26:64). We will never know the precise factors that triggered Judas' remorse, but the evident result was that he threw the money into the temple's inner sanctuary (a provocative act with we know not what intended symbolism) and went out to hang himself.

There are some puzzles here. How is this account reconciled with the version of Judas' death in Acts 1:18–19? And which exact prophetic passages was Matthew thinking of in verses 9–10 (perhaps Zechariah 11:13; Jeremiah 19:1–13; 32:6–9)? Yet Matthew's conviction is clear that all these events were the outworking of God's long-term plan outlined already in scripture. Looking back at 26:24, we see Jesus affirming this conviction, as well as pronouncing his chilling verdict on Judas: 'It would have been better if he had not been born.'

Guidelines

Our readings this week have covered the events of only a few hours—that one long, sleepless night for Jesus during which he walks from the last supper to Gethsemane and then is led back into the city under arrest. Such a lot happens in a short space: this is the strangest and most significant night in the history of humanity. Yet, though much that happens on that fateful night is full of darkness, there is a figure in the midst who is himself full of light. And overhead—throughout that night from sunset to sunrise—there would have been hovering over Jerusalem the bright light of the full Passover moon. Sometimes it can be powerful for us to go out at night ourselves, standing under the gaze of a full moon, and there to ponder how much Jesus went through for us while looking up at that identical sight—the Son of Man looking up at the moon's reflection of the hidden sun.

1 Whose responsibility?

Matthew 27:11–26

Matthew's account, after describing Judas' fate, returns to its focus on Jesus, who is now standing before Pilate (the Roman procurator from AD26 to 36). Almost certainly, this hearing took place in the former palace of King Herod the Great (died 4BC), a far more comfortable place to stay than the Antonia Fortress (the soldiers' barracks overlooking the temple). Pilate would have conducted the trial on a raised platform or 'judgment seat' (v. 19).

Matthew (like Mark) takes us straight to the point when Pilate asks Jesus, 'Are you the King of the Jews?' This shows how the religious leaders have already translated the Jewish term 'Messiah' (used by Matthew in verses 17 and 22, whereas Mark 15:9 and 12 still use 'King') into political categories that will make sense to Pilate. There were clearly many other smaller charges (vv. 13–14), but this was the 'killer' point.

The amnesty offered to Barabbas is ironic. He, not Jesus, was the political freedom-fighter whose hostility Pilate should have been worried about; Jesus ends up accused of being the very thing he was not—an anti-Roman 'Zealot'. There is also the irony that if Jesus really was this political Messiah, which is what many in the 'crowd' were longing for, why did they not want him to be released in order that he might lead their cause? So the very fact that the leaders cajoled the crowd to choose Barabbas in itself revealed that the leaders, despite their charges, knew that Jesus was not such a political leader. Pilate's question to the crowd thus brilliantly revealed some of the leaders' true motivations—especially 'envy' (v. 18).

Yet the situation also puts him in a dilemma: his wife (Claudia Procula) is convinced that Jesus is 'innocent' (v. 19) and he himself knows the political charge is false, but the crowd is now turning nasty, baying for Jesus' blood. Matthew does not absolve Pilate of all responsibility: there probably were some other options (could Jesus not have been kept under Roman guard, as Paul was in Acts 22—27?), so weak Pilate is acting wrongly. No amount of 'hand-washing' changes that.

Yet, for Matthew, the primary responsibility for Jesus' death resides with the 'chief priests and elders', who, when the crowd was vacillating, were already intent on destroying Jesus (v. 20). This narrows somewhat the otherwise sweeping reference to 'all the people' (v. 25), as does the fact that there were probably under 100 people in that early morning crowd. Nevertheless, Matthew, writing as a Jew himself, does see something deeply symbolic and decisive in this act in which God's own chosen people effectively reject their own God-given king.

2 Mockery and darkness

Matthew 27:27–44

Jesus is delivered over to crucifixion (v. 26). What happens next, we know well: mockery by the soldiers (vv. 27–31), a random person from North Africa being asked to carry Jesus' cross-beam out through the city gate to Golgotha (vv. 32–33), Jesus' brave refusal of any drink to ease the pain (v. 34) and then the cruel act of the crucifixion itself—nails being driven through Jesus' wrist and ankle bones.

Matthew (as, indeed, do all the Gospel writers) spares us the gory details of being crucified: most in his audience would have been all too familiar with this Roman punishment for slaves and political rebels. Yet his reticence should not blind us to the utter horror of this familiar scene and the excruciating pain inflicted on Jesus. Around polite Roman dinner tables you were not allowed to mention the word 'cross': it was recognised as too obscene and barbaric.

For Jewish victims, there were two extra insults. Not only did the Old Testament include the teaching that anyone 'hung on a tree' was under a divine curse (Deuteronomy 21:23; see Galatians 3:13), but there was also the Jewish horror of nakedness in public (in contrast to the Greeks, for example, whose athletic competitions were regularly performed in the nude). It is most unlikely that the Romans in Judea bowed to Jewish scruples at this point, so crucified victims were presumably stripped of all their clothing—as Matthew may be delicately hinting in verse 35.

Matthew's own focus seems to be on the outrageous mockery to which Jesus is subjected by the guards in Pilate's headquarters, by general passers-by, by the religious leaders and even by his fellow victims (though see Luke 23:40–43), all of it not just cruel and unkind but profoundly untrue and wrong. They jest about his kingship, placing a crown of thorns on his head, but this man is a king (the title on his cross, even if also a mocking title, is profoundly true). They might taunt him with claiming to rebuild the temple 'in three days', but in three days' time he will do just that in the resurrection of the 'temple' of his body (John 2:20–21). And, yes, he has 'saved others', but the means by which he is going to save millions more is not to save himself and come down from the cross, but to stay there. All this requires from Jesus an incredible 'trust in God' (v. 43). Ultimately God 'delivered' and vindicated him, but at this precise moment all appears grim and bleak. It is the world's darkest day.

3 Darkness and awe

Matthew 27:45–56

The darkness of the crucifixion is now expressed in a physical way. There was discussion in the first Christian centuries about whether this darkness could have been caused by an eclipse; astronomically, however, that is impossible at the time of full moon, so more probably it was a severe desert sandstorm, causing the Jerusalem area to be covered in an eerie grey light. In any event, the darkness was entirely fitting, for this was the moment when Jesus was 'driving out the ruler of this world' (John 12:31), or, as Paul puts it, 'disarming the rulers and authorities' in the spiritual world (Colossians 2:15). Jesus is fighting solo in a cosmic battle; evil is doing its worst.

At the same time, Jesus is also entering into God's wrath. Thus his cry from the cross, 'My God, why have you forsaken me?' (v. 46), almost certainly means more than just that Jesus felt abandoned by God, although that would be true enough in these dire circumstances. Rather, in some profound way that we will never fathom, he was truly abandoned by God—separated from his Father as he willingly 'bore our sin' on which God's judgment fell (1 Peter 2:24; 2 Corinthians 5:21).

In seeking to see the full meaning of Jesus' crucifixion, we inevitably begin to draw on the later theological insights of other New Testament writers, as God revealed to them what Jesus had done. At the actual time, none of those insights were obvious, and the Gospel writers (because they were writing Gospels with narratives, not epistles with theology) decided not to weave theological commentary into their account of the crucifixion. Even so, there are clear signs that Matthew wants us to derive these theological truths from his narrative.

Note, then, the rending of the temple veil (v. 51), indicating that access into God's holy presence is now possible through the atonement for sin accomplished by Jesus. Note the (unparalleled) account of the saints being raised (vv. 52–53), a clear sign that Jesus' death (not just his resurrection) is a defining moment when death itself is being overturned. Note the earthquake (v. 51), a sign that we are dealing with cosmic, earth-shattering events. This is indeed a unique moment, the axle on which human history turns, such that the world will never be the same again.

Overall, Matthew's account is distinguished by a sense of awe, for this was indeed no ordinary death but the death of the unique Son of God. It was truly, then, an awe-filled, awesome event, in response to which we should ourselves be awestruck and shaken to the core of our beings.

4 Burial

Matthew 27:57–66

One of the surprising silences in this story concerns Jesus' male disciples. Where are they? Matthew records that those who witnessed Jesus' death included 'many women' who had followed him from Galilee (v. 55); he then talks about Joseph of Arimathea, who was also in the wider circle of Jesus' disciples (v. 57). We know from John's Gospel that the 'beloved disciple' was at the scene (19:26–27), but otherwise the male followers are totally absent. Peter is somewhere in the city, hiding in shame, and the others are probably on the far side of the Mount of Olives, hiding in Bethany.

In later years, it must have been slightly embarrassing for these disciples to admit that they had missed the key event. The Gospel writers never draw explicit attention to their cowardly absence; nor is it ever used as an argument why they, as opposed to the women, should not occupy leading roles; but note how implicitly Matthew will use the great commission as a means of reinstating the 'eleven disciples' and confirming them as Jesus' intended leaders of his new community (28:16).

Meanwhile, the women (who, though no threat to the local authorities and therefore reasonably safe, were also pretty much powerless to do anything for Jesus) will have been very grateful for Joseph's intervention at this point. Without it, there was a high risk that Jesus' body would be thrown by the Roman soldiers into a common grave; now, at least, there was an opportunity for his corpse to be given a hasty burial, and there was a job that they *could* do for Jesus after the sabbath—returning to perform a more proper burial.

For the Jewish leaders, however, Joseph's intervention was thoroughly annoying. It meant that the custody of Jesus' corpse became clearly a Jewish responsibility, not a Roman one. Hence their urgent return to Pilate the next day, in an attempt to clarify the lines of responsibility. Pilate's response ('You have a guard', v. 65, NRSV) is now regrettably ambiguous: is he offering to supply some of his Roman soldiers or instead requiring the Jewish leaders to deploy some of their temple guards? Either way, as the Saturday comes to a close, the stage has now been set by Matthew as follows:

- There is a guarded tomb, with its whereabouts well known to at least two women among Jesus' followers (v. 61).
- The tomb has a sealed entrance, which will prove very difficult for the women, when returning, to open.
- Inside the tomb is the corpse of a man who has been heard, even by his enemies, to claim that he will 'rise after three days'.

The tension mounts: what will happen next?

5 Resurrection and worship

Matthew 28:1–10

Answer: the resurrection! In a mighty act of God, Jesus' physical corpse is raised to new life: 'He has risen, just as he said!' (v. 6). The tragic events of the previous few days, when forces in Jerusalem had conspired to do away with this messianic pretender, are now overturned by a unique event that only confirms his Messiahship. For Jesus' followers in Jerusalem on that day, despair turns to hope, uncontrollable grief to unstoppable joy (v. 8). Jesus, their master, is alive!

For Matthew, this is the great climax of his Gospel. To be honest, it hardly comes as a total surprise to his readers—not just because Jesus predicted it on several occasions, but also because Matthew's Jesus has been such an authoritative figure. His miracles have been awesome, his teaching as authoritative as God's revealed Law; he has been called the 'Lord' and the 'Son of God', even 'God with us'; on two occasions he has been 'worshipped' (2:11; 14:33). For a Jewish writer like Matthew, this clearly means that Jesus is being identified in some way with God, because only God was to be worshipped (as affirmed by Jesus himself in Matthew 4:10, quoting Deuteronomy 6:13). Now, with Jesus' resurrection, this worship comes to full fruition: 'They... took hold of his feet, and worshipped him' (v. 9; see also v. 17).

Matthew's account of the resurrection is thus presented to us as a dramatic theophany—a revelation of God in his awesome power and majesty, not unlike that given to the Israelites at Sinai. So, before the women arrived, there had been a great earthquake (27:51) and the arrival of an 'angel of the Lord' who had been sitting authoritatively on the rolling-stone and whose appearance sent shuddering fear into those who saw him (vv. 4, 5, 8). The actual moment of Jesus' resurrection is never described by the Gospel writers because it was never seen (when the women arrive, the tomb is already empty), yet Matthew has helped us to sense how dramatic it must have been and introduces us skilfully into its seismic 'aftershocks'.

Jesus' resurrection means, of course, that the one raised on the first Easter Day continues as a living reality into the present. Matthew wanted his readers not just to contemplate this historical event in the past but to be drawn into encounter with the risen Jesus themselves—for him to walk off the pages and into their lives. This can be true for us, too. 'Jesus met them' (v. 9) and he can meet us; and, when we encounter him, our response can only be one of 'worship'.

6 Cover-up and restoration

Matthew 28:11–20

All now is confusion among those in Jerusalem who are connected to Jesus—the women running to the male disciples with the great news; the guards running to the chief priests with the (for them) terrible news. Another emergency Sanhedrin council meeting is called and the only workable solution to the problem is agreed upon—bribery, deceit and mutual cover-up. Anything but the truth!

Matthew is the only Gospel writer to mention the setting of the guards at the tomb (27:64–66). For him, this helps to highlight the dramatic nature of the resurrection (which the guards were powerless to withstand); yet it also serves to explain the source of the rumour about Jesus' body being stolen by his disciples (v. 15). In a sense, this accusation was the only line of argument that could be advanced. No one was going to suggest some of the modern attempted explanations (for example, that the women went to the wrong tomb or that Jesus did not truly die). Such crude alternatives would have been knowingly ludicrous at the time. Yet Matthew asserts that the rumour was started by the desperate guards—having, shamefacedly, to admit to having been asleep at the moment the crime was committed. It's all starting to sound rather implausible!

This brief final chapter, however, now skips to the one event which, for Matthew, neatly summarises the whole story: Jesus' promised rendezvous with his disciples back in Galilee (26:32; 28:7, 10). No doubt he knew of other resurrection appearances in Jerusalem, but this one said it all:

• Jesus' male disciples are restored and forgiven in their home area, and on a 'mountain' or hillside above the lake—similar (or even identical?) to the one where they first heard Jesus' authoritative teaching (5:1).

- Jesus announces his total authority, requiring total obedience to his teaching, and commissions the making of more disciples, not only in Judea but among 'all nations'.
- Jesus promises to be always with his people—truly 'God with us' (see 1:23).

This is indeed a powerful ending to the whole Gospel. So many of the themes that Matthew has highlighted come to a climax here: the importance of discipleship, the reality of Jesus as God's Son and of his Spirit, his eternal nature and unequalled authority, and his divine presence. Matthew want us his readers, as it were, to join with those first disciples on the hillside, to affirm our own commitment and, having grasped these incredible truths, to play our part also in being sent out to others with the news that can change the waiting world.

Guidelines

The resurrection of Jesus—though briefly covered by Matthew in just one quite short chapter—comes as the great, crashing climax of the whole Gospel. There has been, in Matthew's compressed account, so much teaching, but now we are given this powerful and dramatic activity of God. It reminds us that, undergirding the whole Gospel and beneath all of Jesus' teaching and acts of power, there has been the powerful hand of the living God. The earthquake of 28:2 thus matches the deeper reality that this world has been invaded by divine power and that we are witnessing, literally, 'earth-shattering' events. So we are supposed, like the guards, to be 'shaken' and disturbed—to have our worldviews shattered and overturned by this Jesus-story. Then we are meant to go out into the world, ourselves changed; and, newly equipped with the teachings of Jesus as summarised by Matthew, to 'teach others to obey everything' he has taught. Out we go!

Psalms 51 (50)—63 (62)

The Psalter is the prayer book of Israel and expresses the full range of human emotion, pulling no punches. In this group of 13 psalms, we are given the opportunity to reflect on our confidence in God's grace, sovereignty and loving-kindness even as we are confronted by violent enemies and treacherous friends. The psalmists do not ignore the instinct to strike back against evil and seek retribution, but they turn continually to God as the one in whom to seek refuge ad sanctuary.

These notes are based on the Revised Grail Psalter and, unless otherwise stated, on the New Jerusalem Bible.

A note on numbering: The Revised Grail Psalter, in accordance with the Roman Catholic tradition, uses the numbering of the Greek version of the Psalms, rather than the Hebrew. In the Greek text, the Hebrew Psalms 9 and 10 are shown as a single psalm—Psalm 9. Thus the Greek version stays one number behind until Psalm 148. Because many Protestant versions adopt the Hebrew numbering (following Luther's preference), however, both numbers have been given in psalm references between 10 and 147. You will find the Hebrew number given first, with the Greek in brackets afterwards.

26 September–2 October

1 Have mercy on me, O God

Psalm 51 (50)

This is the best-known and best-loved of the seven penitential psalms. The caption added later to the psalm associates it with David's repentance after his adultery with Bathsheba and his dastardly attempt to cover up his sin by bringing her husband Uriah home from the battlefield (and then having him killed). There is nothing in the psalm itself to attach it to this incident. Indeed, the final pair of verses reflects the period of the rebuilding of the temple after the return from exile, and the concern of that period about legitimate sacrifice. However, these two verses may well have been added, for the body of the psalm sets conversion above sacrifice.

The main body of the psalm falls into two halves, each in a chiasmus or Chinese-box pattern. It would be tedious to follow this out in detail, but the first half is bracketed by 'blot out… wash me… cleanse me' (vv. 1–2) and 'cleanse me… wash me… blot out' (vv. 7–9). It centres on confession of sin and awareness of inexcusable guilt: 'you are just in your sentence' (v. 4). The second half is bracketed by 'heart… spirit' (v. 10) and 'spirit… heart' (v. 17). It centres on God's salvation (vv. 12, 14) and the return of sinners. As the spirituality of the first half chimes in with the consciousness of sin and guilt in Jeremiah, so the second half is enriched by the teaching on a new heart and new spirit in the promises of Ezekiel. After the disastrous infidelities that led to the Babylonian exile, Israel will be endowed with a new heart—a heart of flesh instead of a heart of stone—and the spirit or breath of life (Ezekiel 36:26; 37:5). This is the joy of salvation, or the saving joy, which the psalmist will announce to sinners.

The real warmth of the psalm comes from the first three words. The opening word, translated 'Have mercy on me', is formed from the same word as for a mother's womb. It is a plea for the unbreakable love of a mother, which can never be denied to her children, whatever they may do—the affinity engendered by the mother carrying her baby for nine loving and expectant months in the womb. The third word, translated 'your merciful love' (yes, all one word in the Hebrew), appeals to the inviolable family loyalty between members of the same family: I may find my brother difficult and obstinate, but, when push comes to shove, I won't let him down.

2 Why do you boast of wickedness?

Psalms 52 (51) and 53 (52)

Psalm 52 (51) is the first of three little psalms in which the psalmist is set against evil and powerful opponents. There is, however, no need to attach it to Doeg the Edomite, as the superscription does. Doeg ratted on David by telling Saul that David had purloined from the sanctuary the show-bread and Goliath's sword; but Doeg was a mere herdsman, not a champion (1 Samuel 21:1–10; 22:9–10).

The structure of this psalm falls neatly into three sections. The first (vv. 1–4) sharply and sarcastically badmouths the champion of evil. The second (vv. 5–7) shows us the righteous smugly and merrily laughing at the discomfiture and uprooting of this champion who trusted in his own prowess.

The third section (vv. 8–9) reverses the image of the uprooting of the braggart champion of evil by likening the psalmist to a growing olive tree in the house of God. The braggart is uprooted, the psalmist is deep-rooted; the braggart trusts in his own strength, the psalmist in the name of the Lord. The olive is a slow-growing tree, the very symbol of stability. It may take 30 years to reach its full fruiting capacity but will then continue to bear fruit for most of a millennium if it is tended with loving care, the sort of care an olive tree will receive in the house of God. Today many olive trees stand as a reminder on the Temple Mount, the area where the temple once stood. To harm a neighbour's olive tree is considered a heinous crime. The rape of olive orchards by governmental shifting of borders (for example, around Bethlehem) rankles more deeply with the Palestinians than almost any other hurt.

So, in Jeremiah 11:16, Israel is named by the Lord 'Green olive-tree covered in fine fruit'. In Romans 11, Paul again uses this figure in his consideration of the agonising enigma that Israel, so long prepared, has failed to respond to its Messiah. The Jews are the dead branches, cut off to make room for the ingrafting of the shoots of the wild olive, the Gentiles. But by some horticultural miracle ('How rich and deep are the wisdom and the knowledge of God! We cannot reach to the root of his decisions': Romans 11:33), the discarded branches will be grafted back in again in the fullness of time.

Psalm 53 (52) is an almost exact repeat of Psalm 14 (13). It uses the common noun 'God' as the name for the deity, whereas the earlier psalm uses the name YHWH, which is too intimate and too awesome to be pronounced. Apart from this, there are only slight variations in the description of the fate of the wicked in verse 5.

3 O God, save me by your name

This last of the three successive little psalms about opposition falls neatly into two halves: the problem and the solution. The solution unfolds in just the same steps as the problem folded up:

Verse 1: Your name
> Verse 3a: The proud
>> Verse 3b: My life
>>> Verse 3c: They have no regard for God
>>> Verse 4a: I have God for my help
>> Verse 4b: My life
> Verse 5: My foes

Verses 6–7: Your name

How can a name, even the name of God, save? In biblical thought, the giving of a name is a serious matter. Adam completes the creation of the animals by giving them names, thus turning a formless hulk into something that can be grasped and recognised—a lion or mosquito or whatever (Genesis 2:19). When the river sprite, having wrestled with Jacob, gives him the new name of 'Israel', he converts him from being a trickster who has cheated his father, brother and uncle into being a respectable patriarch, the 'Man Seeing God' (Ish-Ra-El: Genesis 32:29). Jesus gives the leader of his disciples the new name of 'Rock', that he may be the foundation of his Church (Matthew 16:18). Most significant of all, Moses is given the special, unpronounceable name of God, but only later is given its meaning as 'a God of tenderness and mercy' (Exodus 34:6). In one psalm after another, God's name is something that provides shelter and security.

In the New Testament, and more particularly in the Acts of the Apostles, the name of Jesus, which means 'Saviour', takes on the same significance. Christians are defined as those who call on the name of Jesus as a security and protection, almost as a sort of talisman. Christians are baptised in the name—that is, in the power—of Jesus. They are also sometimes said to be baptised into the name of Jesus—that is, into the company of Jesus—thereby taking on a solidarity and participation with

Jesus. Christians are also called those over whom the name of Jesus has been pronounced in blessing. In modern spirituality, perhaps especially in the Eastern Churches, this emphasis issues in the Jesus Prayer: 'Lord Jesus Christ, Son of God, have mercy on me.'

4 Give ear, O God, to my prayer

Psalm 55 (54)

This psalm is so varied that it is difficult to characterise. Clearly it is a psalm of lament, laying before the Lord the trouble that the psalmist is undergoing, but is the trouble a personal or a public difficulty? At times it seems personal ('my heart is stricken'); at times the danger seems public ('I see violence and strife in the city'). At times the enemies seem many ('those who fight me are many'), at times the central tragedy seems to be betrayal by a particular friend ('my friend whom I knew so well'). Perhaps the best solution is the suggestion that the poem has grown and expanded as it was used on several occasions, just as the writings of the prophets—perhaps especially the book of Isaiah—were used and reused, with slight adjustments to different contemporary situations. This would be typical of the development of oral tradition.

I am especially moved by two aspects. The first is the longing for the peace of the desert in verses 6–8. Israel always looked back with longing to the peace of the desert, the idyll of simple fidelity to the Lord during the wanderings of the exodus, the honeymoon period. The starkness of the deserts to the east and south of Jerusalem, the Judean desert and the Negeb, has an enduring attraction for the people with its nomadic past. These are gently rolling hills of buff-coloured rock, devoid of all but an occasional wisp of grass, where even the wild camels find little to crop. ('What does the camel find to eat?' I asked. 'The camel, he eat the ground,' replied the diminutive goatherd.) The stillness has a daunting majesty that both scares and elevates the soul. One can appreciate why Jesus went out into the desert after his baptism: he was with the wild beasts, and the angels ministered to him. One can appreciate, too, why the psalmist longed to escape his enemies and take refuge in the silent solitude of the desert.

The other moving aspect is the treachery of the trusted friend in verses 12–14 and 20–21, which the psalmist finds so hard to bear. The Christian cannot but be reminded of Judas. Jesus trusted him to the extent of making him the cashier of the group of disciples. Or was the triple denial by Peter, the 'Rock', in his hour of need, a more devastating betrayal? And what of my own betrayals?

5 In God I trust, I shall not fear

Psalm 56 (55)

The shape of this poem of fear and trust is straightforward. It has two parts (vv. 1–7 and 8–13), each anchored in the central refrain of invincible confidence in God's power to solve the problem (vv. 4, 10–11). Each half also ends with a firm statement of confidence (vv. 7, 12–13). Perhaps the most striking feature of the psalm is the repeated combination of fear and trust. The one never appears without the other, but the two are always together, balancing one another.

The psalm raises in sharp form the question, 'Who are these enemies?' There is mention of assailants and ambush, of rescue from death and of the foes turning back. These elements suggest real armed attack. But there is mention also of pride and verbal distortion by the enemies—a non-violent, verbal attack. Allied to this is the question, 'Who is represented as praying?' Commentators often place this and other such psalms in the mouth of a king, beleaguered by the armies of national enemies. This would place the psalms at the time of the Davidic monarchy, when kings engaged in both petty and major wars. Are we to believe that they took time off to compose such prayers, or that such prayers were ready to hand for them in the temple? While it seems most probable that the collection of psalms stems from the temple, we have no idea how it was formed or housed. In any case, the weight of scholarly opinion is that the majority of the psalms were composed during the Second Temple period, after the restoration from exile in Babylon, when kings (if they existed) played a much less prominent role.

In the course of the psalms, enemies are presented in a variety of guises, as packs of dogs roaming about the city, fierce bulls of Bashan, the horns of wild oxen, floods of water reaching high, nets or traps laid in the path, enemies patrolling the city walls night and day. If taken literally, these images would suggest an endemically violent, brutal and unstable society—an impression not borne out by the rest of biblical literature. It is better to understand these threats as vivid metaphors: 'their teeth are spears and arrows, their tongue a sharpened sword' (Psalm 57:4). In prayer we know our own fallibility and proneness to be lured or scared from the right path. This psalm's combination of fear and trust is no bad image for the tightrope we walk.

6 Be exalted, O God, above the heavens!

Psalm 57 (56)

This psalm betrays the same context as the previous psalm in the collection, a balance between hostile threats and confidence in God. It falls into two halves, each concluding with the refrain, 'Be exalted above the heavens, O God; above all the earth is your glory' (vv. 5, 11). This gives the clue to a difference in this psalm compared with the previous one: it includes a cosmic dimension, involving not only the heavens but also the nations on earth. Correspondingly, it is no longer on the knife-edge, poised between fear on the one side and trust on the other, but is full of confidence and praise.

What are we to do with 'the heavens' in an age when a three-decker universe is out of fashion? It is no longer useful to conceive of God 'up there' in deist isolation. We concentrate much more on divine interpenetration of all things, the divine presence conserving creation from moment to moment. The idea of the heavens can, however, still contribute to this conception. 'Your love reaches to the heavens and your truth to the skies' (v. 10; see also v. 3) suggests the spread of these two divine influences, two divine ways of communicating with us—love and truth—right from us into the limitless, expanding universe. They fill the intervening space, and even the cyberspace as well!

This impression is confirmed by the final concentration in each half of the psalm on the divine glory. That wonderful concept of divine glory, both thrilling and awesome, reverses the movement, spreading not from earth as far as heaven but from heaven to earth, again filling the intervening space. So in the shadow of his wings I am wrapped not only in love and truth but also in the divine glory.

Another aspect of the cosmic dimension is the inclusion of the nations in the praise of God (v. 9). The Babylonian exile alerted Israel to other nations, who worshipped other gods, and to the question of how these nations were to be saved, since Israel saw more and more strongly that there was only one true God. The answer was that they were to be saved by Israel's God, and were to come to Jerusalem to draw salvation from there. So Israel becomes the focus for universal salvation. The nations, too, will draw waters from the wells of salvation, and will come bringing gifts to Israel's God. In the preparation for the gospel message to all nations, this becomes ever clearer, until in Zechariah 14 we have the great scene of the assize of all nations on the Mount of Olives: 'When that Day comes, the Lord will be the one and only and his name the one name' (v. 14).

Guidelines

In most of the psalms of this group, the psalmist prays earnestly for the discomfiture of his enemies. Indeed, he exults in the certainty of it! What are we to do about this? In some cases these verses are frankly omitted. In other versions, to maintain the integrity of the scriptures, such passages are walled off by square brackets, so that even if they are read they are not read aloud.

Perhaps a better solution is to face up to the advance of revelation. The morals of the Old Testament assume the acceptability of vengeance. Moreover, 'an eye for an eye and a tooth for a tooth' was an advance from a more primitive morality, limiting revenge to a balance with the offence. It was not until the teaching of Jesus that revenge was wholly outlawed. Jesus teaches in one parable after another, as well as by his own actions, the difficult lesson that human beings, made in the image of God, must image also God's unconditional forgiveness. It's a lesson not easily learned, even by those of us who call ourselves Christians. How unusual the case, and how precious the lesson, of those who truly forgive when a loved one is lost in sectarian or other violence!

1 Do you truly speak justice?

Psalm 58 (57)

This is one of the very few psalms not generally used in the public liturgy. It is used neither in the Roman Breviary nor in the Common Lectionary. This is less because the text is highly corrupt, and is reconstructed in very different ways, than because it is lusciously vindictive.

Judges hold the divine power of judgment, and all public judgment should echo and prolong the judgment of God. The Law consistently teaches that if Israel is to be the people of God, it must treat the widow, the stranger and the orphan as God himself treated the Israelites when they were strangers in Egypt—but this did not always happen. In a less strictly controlled system of justice, the rich had plenty of opportunity to make themselves richer through the administration of justice, instead of righting injustice. From the earliest prophets onwards, Amos, Hosea and the other messengers of God's word constantly reproached the rich for misusing their power as judges and administrators, falsifying weights and measures to their own advantage, accepting bribes and so on. This psalm joins its voice to theirs. The problem, indeed, persists. There are plenty of situations in the modern world, even in Christian countries, where injustice is officially done and the downtrodden have no hope of redress.

However, in the psalm, wicked judges are vituperated in terms that go far beyond modern political correctness, almost as though the author is delighting in his colourful vituperation for its own sake. Liturgists no doubt felt that the terms were too violent to be edifying or prayerful. The same is true of the splendidly constructed and detailed curse in the most famous of all Cursing Psalms, Psalm 109 (108). These unjust judges are first described in the most colourful terms as venomous snakes refusing to obey the snake charmer: evidently the African horned viper was considered to be deaf because it has no visible hearing apparatus. Then their retribution is described in terms of extreme and pitiless violence: teeth broken in the mouth, snails dissolving into slime. The psalm ends on a note of satisfaction, with the righteous bathing their feet in the blood of the wicked.

2 Rescue me, God, from my foes

Psalm 59 (58)

The violence of this psalm is its most striking feature—both the threatening violence of the psalmist's enemies and the violence that he prays his God to visit upon them. We do not know the context of this energetic and colourful prayer, but hints allow us at least to imagine a context for it. The basis of it is spatial: at the centre is the psalmist, clinging to his divine Protector, his Strength, his God in whom he trusts. He makes an urgent plea for protection, coupled with insistent protestations of innocence (vv. 3–4). In the background is an encircling miasma of predatory beasts, twice described as howling like dogs as they roam about the city each evening (vv. 6, 14–15). The psalmist veers between praying for their violent and merciless annihilation and mitigating his plea to a request that they be allowed to remain as a reminder of God's protective power while God merely laughs at them.

The context may be imagined (but with no certainty) as the biblical institution of sanctuary. Joshua 20 makes provision for six cities of refuge, scattered throughout the promised land, to which an unintentional killer may flee for sanctuary. In the rough system of justice practised in those days (and still among the local Arab tribes), the family of the killed man was obliged to exact vengeance from the killer, regardless of blame. The killer could take refuge in these cities until a trial before the community could be sorted out. However, this privilege may have been more notional than real. The only recorded instance of its successful use seems to have been Adonijah's flight to the altar in fear of Solomon's anger (1 Kings 1:50). Soon afterwards, the veteran general Joab, a supporter of Adonijah, attempted to use the same privilege. But he was too formidable an opponent to be allowed to live, and Solomon audaciously had him cut down at the altar itself (1 Kings 2:28–34).

In medieval times, churches provided sanctuary from arrest under some conditions, and even in modern society the same appeal to divine protection has occasionally been successful, principally in cases of illegal immigration. This is a moving case of residual respect for the protective power of the divinity (however this divinity may be envisaged) as at least a guarantee of fair play in a professedly post-Christian world. How much more assured in the world of the psalmist was the protection of the Lord against these raiders of the night!

3 With God we shall do bravely

Psalm 60 (59)

The attitude expressed by this psalm could be described as 'confidence in defeat'. The first section (vv. 1–4) characterises a military defeat in the apocalyptic terms of an earthquake. The use of such language in Hebrew poetry is frequent. Nor is it absent from sports journalism in English! Drinking a cup is a frequent image of swallowing some bitterness— 'taking the medicine' (Isaiah 51:17, 20–21)—used of course also by Jesus to the sons of Zebedee (Mark 10:38–39) and in his own agony in Gethsemane (Mark 14:36).

Immediately after this unpromising start, the psalmist launches paradoxically into confident claims for various parts of the territory distributed by Joshua. First, two cities of northern Israel, Shechem and Succoth, are claimed for God. This suggests that the psalm was written in Judah after the return from exile, when the northern kingdom was in the hands of foreigners, the Samaritans. Then larger northern territories, Gilead and Manasseh, are claimed. Finally Ephraim (just north of Jerusalem) and Judah itself are claimed. The status of these two areas is different, for Ephraim has the dignity of being the helmet of the Lord, while Judah has the highest prize, as God's own sceptre. In contrast to the others, both these mentions may well be complimentary.

Next the psalmist turns to the traditional enemies of Israel. The Philistines had been the main enemies in the early period, increasingly encroaching on Israel until defeated and repulsed by King David. Then they virtually ceased to exist, although they gave their name to the country of 'Palestine'. After this the psalmist turns to two large territories east of the Jordan which had constantly been thorns in Israel's flesh. Moab had taken part in the plundering of Jerusalem at the time of the exile; it is to be no more than God's washbowl. The worst of the traditional enemies was Edom, against whom there had been constant wars; God's casting his shoe on Edom must be an insulting gesture of appropriation, though there is no real biblical parallel for this figure.

After these brave claims, the psalmist seems to lose confidence again, asking whether God has, after all, rejected Israel and begging for God's help against the enemy. The psalm need not necessarily be regarded as belligerent, for there is no talk of violent destruction of the enemy. It should rather been seen as a statement of God's sovereignty over the whole earth and the whole universe.

4 My refuge and my mighty tower

Psalm 61 (60)

This is a simple little psalm of confidence. It falls into two halves, articulated round the verb 'hear'. This is more obvious in the Hebrew. The first four verses begin with the cry 'Hear, O God!' and make a confident request that God will hear the psalmist's prayer. The second four (vv. 5–8) begin 'You, O God, have heard' and spell out the blessings of which the psalmist is confident. So the first half constitutes the request, the second the fulfilment of that request.

This makes more sense than other emphases. Some commentators stress the cry 'from the end of the earth' (v. 2) and attribute the psalm to a singer in the first deportation to Babylon, while a king was still on the throne of Jerusalem. Others are drawn by the mention of the king (v. 6) to make the king the singer of the psalm—speaking of himself in the third person.

Two details are particularly attractive. The first is 'the rock too high for me to reach' (v. 2). This plays on a characteristic feature of the Holy Land. Among its amazing variety of landscapes is a series of high and rocky peaks, cut off by unassailable cliffs and crowned by castles of many ages—prehistoric, Canaanite, Herodian (King Herod was a great builder), Crusader. Well might the psalmist pray to be set on one of these impregnable peaks as a tower against the foe! Before the invention of gunpowder, they were a refuge that no enemy could penetrate.

The second detail is the messianic prayer for the king (v. 7). There is a sure allusion here to the promises given by the prophet Nathan to David (2 Samuel 7): his heirs will be enthroned for ever before God. Their throne will be founded on and guaranteed by the family love or paternal love (*hesed*) of God, and by God's unfailing fidelity to his promises. These promises were never fulfilled by the line of kings in the Old Testament. Instead, the prophets continued to look forward to their fulfilment in the Messiah whom God would send to bring the kingship of God to completion at the end of time. We see them to be fulfilled in Jesus the Christ. As the prologue to the Gospel of John concludes, 'The Law came through Moses, grace and truth through Jesus Christ' (John 1:17). 'Grace and truth' are the family love and the fulfilment promised in this psalm.

5 In God alone is my soul at rest

Psalm 62 (61)

We can divide this psalm into three sections. The first two begin with a sort of refrain (vv. 1–2, 5–6), identical in the two cases but for one crucial exception: the first refrain sees God as the source of salvation, the second as the source of hope. These two key words provide enough to meditate on for the course of the whole psalm. Both are the basis of any stability.

'Salvation' often carries an allusion to the events of the past, to the exodus from Egypt, when God delivered his people from the misery of slavery and the perils of pursuit, and again to the deliverance from captivity in Babylon. But for the Christian the sense is further enriched because the name 'Jesus' is the same word in Hebrew. For us, the concept of salvation is captured by and focused on Jesus. He is the Saviour, and in him God the Saviour brings his ancient work of salvation to completion. For a Christian, the idea of 'hope', the second key word of the refrains, is also no vague concept. It is the confidence in things to come. The letter to the Hebrews is the most burning scriptural expression of hope, with its deep conviction of pilgrimage; it sees the people of God journeying restlessly to the place of rest promised to them but never reached in the Old Testament (Hebrews 4:1–13).

After each of these two initial refrains comes a comment. The first (vv. 3–4) is negative, describing the attack of enemies on God's faithful one as though he were (splendid images!) 'a tottering wall or a tumbling fence'. The second (vv. 7–8) is positive, a joyful confirmation of the refrain, full of strong and positive words: 'salvation', 'glory', 'strength' and 'refuge'.

The third section of the psalm is quite different and is the first occurrence for some time of a Wisdom passage. The Wisdom literature is always instructional, reflecting on life and humanity, on human capacities and follies. In the days towards the end of the Old Testament period, when there seemed to be no more prophets to guide God's people, great collections of Wisdom sayings and proverbs were made, which found their way into the collection of writings we now call the Bible. The last section of this psalm (vv. 9–12) is just such a little collection of reflections. It has a lovely build-up. Verse 9 starts with the inanity of human powers. The key word is *hebel*, which features so prominently in the book of Ecclesiastes: 'vanity of vanities', a mere breath—passing, swiftly dissipated and utterly forgotten. Verse 10 paints the consequences: no human wealth or plunder can satisfy. Then verse 11 comes crashing in with the opposite, the power of God and his love, which really are effective.

6 My soul thirsts for God

Psalm 63 (62)

This yearning psalm is the climax of a set of three. Psalm 61 (60) was a prayer of quiet confidence that God would hear the psalmist's prayer. Psalm 62 (61) is suffused with the themes of hope and salvation. Now we have a picture of the psalmist secure in attachment to the Lord. The tenses of the Hebrew verbs used here imply a continuous state of seeking, thirsting, pining. This is no temporary state but the condition that is the foundation of the psalmist's being—confident attachment to God—so that 'thirsts' and 'pines' better yield the sense of the original than 'is thirsting' and 'is pining'.

I once got lost in the Judean desert, crossing it from Jerusalem to the Dead Sea with two strapping young friends. It was my own silly fault in map-reading. We ran out of water and really knew what 'a dry, weary land without water' (v. 1) meant. Just as we were stumbling to a standstill, the Lord provided a jeep out of nowhere. It is then that one realises the blessing of water, and even perceives the 'strength and glory' of God. Although the psalmist has come before God 'in the holy place', the place is not important, for he nestles with God at the banquet and also through the night watches, permanently enjoying the presence of God.

For Christians, the banquet immediately suggests the messianic banquet at the end of time, the image so often used by Jesus in his parables of the last times and his sayings about the bridegroom, when God invites (indeed, presses) even sinners to join in the feast. Is there even a suggestion of life after death in 'your love is better than life' (v. 3)? We find the same thought in Paul: 'Life to me, of course, is Christ, but then death would be a positive gain' (Philippians 1:21). At the time of the psalmist, Israel had not yet been granted the full revelation of life after death, but is this already a hint, a suggestion that the love of God is so intense that it survives even physical death? Job had already proclaimed in his suffering, 'I know that after my awakening he will set me close to him' (Job 19:26). God will not let go of all those whom he loves, for 'he is God not of the dead but of the living' (Mark 12:27). That makes a fitting climax to these three psalms of confident praise.

Guidelines

This group of psalms has its fair share of violence, of conflict with the enemy. For the psalmists, the enemy appears to be external and physical, but the variety of expression shows, as we have already suggested, that some of the descriptions may be metaphorical. Our own struggle is mostly against ourselves, our own evil tendencies and bad habits. There can be no doubt about this! The forces of evil do exist, but I personally have never seen or touched a force. Forces for good there must be, and these are the watchful and benign powers of God, ever empowering us to good— the smile of God which itself gives ability to follow the right path. It is dangerous if we concretise our evil tendencies and blame them on the forces of evil, the enemy or Satan the tempter. The decisions are ours, but they are made easier if we live in the presence and praise of God.

Revelation

At the very back of the Bible, lurking just before the concordances and the maps, is the book of Revelation, or the Apocalypse as it is sometimes called. Its name is derived from the Greek word *apokalupsis*, meaning to 'unveil' or 'reveal'; and, of all the books of the Bible, this one stands out from the crowd as being somehow different. It is a book of wild imagination, vivid pictures and terrifying visions. It is a book of many-headed beasts, of dragons and angels, of seas of blood, blazing stars, earthquakes and plagues. It is a book ripe for imaginative interpretation. Its place within the Christian scriptures has been heavily debated throughout the history of the Church, as have its date and authorship. Yet it has, nonetheless, been highly influential with readers, preachers and writers who have drawn on the rich, descriptive images and applied them easily to the world in which they live. Sometimes this process has been positive: for Black South Africans struggling against apartheid in the second half of the 20th century, the text brought hope of a better world to come. But sometimes interpreters have used the text in a negative way. David Koresh's Branch Davidian community in Waco, Texas, used the Apocalypse to justify a number of beliefs and practices that led to death, destruction and suffering through catastrophic fire in 1993.

The enduring magnetism and natural appeal of the book of Revelation is due, in part, to the central idea that although we may suffer in this life, it will be for but a moment, as the end of all suffering is coming and is maybe just around the corner. The return of Christ will right all those wrongs and usher in a new age where God shall live with his people and 'wipe every tear from their eyes' (21:4). Yet the hope offered here does not pertain to the distant future only; rather, the author is seeking to reassure his readers in their present experiences. Even though it may look as though the devil has the upper hand, God is really in control behind the scenes. Have you ever suffered? Are you experiencing suffering right now? If so, this strangely compelling book is for you. Take comfort in it!

1 Blessed is he who reads

Revelation 1

What does it mean to have a revelation? It isn't just finding out a new bit of knowledge, discovering something interesting or increasing our understanding. Here John has received a disclosure of supernatural divine truth, which has been conveyed to him by the power of the Holy Spirit, so there is something special about both the content and the conveyance of a revelation that goes beyond mere knowledge or understanding. It's the same with the Christian faith. The Christian faith isn't a hypothesis that we either understand or don't understand. It's not just a good idea or a bit of information. It's a revelation—a disclosure of supernatural divine truth conveyed to us through the power of the Holy Spirit. It is this revelation: Jesus is risen from the dead. He is Lord. He loves us and has freed us from our sin by the shedding of his blood (v. 5). When we realise that, we haven't just increased our theological knowledge: the veil has been removed (*apokalupsis*) and the truth has been revealed (*revelatio*).

But why should we read this strange and mysterious book? Because verse 3 tells us that reading it brings a blessing. There can't be many *Guidelines* notes that make such a grand promise as that on day one! Advertisers are frequently worried about being sued over false advertising: does a product really do what it 'says on the tin'? John guarantees that if we read, hear and do, we will be blessed. Why? Because this reminds us that 'he is coming!' (v. 7). We are reminded that our faith does not just give us, in the words of the hymn, 'strength for today' but also 'bright hope for tomorrow' (T.O. Chisholm).

We are also blessed in the reminder that when we suffer and face hardship, we never do so alone. In verse 13 we see 'the Son of Man' walking 'in the midst' of the churches, and this reminds us that Jesus is not just the Alpha (the 'one who was') or just the Omega (the 'one who is to come') but also the Beta to Psi—in the present, the 'one who is' (vv. 8, 17), who walks with us now, today, in our present sufferings, and says, 'Do not be afraid' (v. 17) for I walk with you.

2 I know your works

Revelation 2:1–11

Prophecy is often understood as predicting, discerning and perceiving future events, yet the predictive element is only one dimension of prophecy. Prophecy also contains a strongly instructive dimension. Consider the prophets of the post-exilic period (586–166BC; for example, Jeremiah and Nehemiah). Their prophecies generally followed the formula, 'If you keep misbehaving, then in the future God will punish you, but if you repent and start behaving yourselves, then in the future God will bless you' (see Jeremiah 3:19—4:3; Nehemiah 1:5–10). Such prophecy is clearly instructive rather than predictive. Prophecy is used here as the imperative for moral behaviour. It is in this chapter that we begin to see something of the moral and ethical dimension of the Revelation: it is prophetically instructive. Indeed, John sees himself as the last in a great line of prophets, starting with Moses, moving through to Malachi and ending with his own vision. John, like those who went before him, uses prophecy not just to predict but to instruct—to call people to right moral living.

Here John begins his prophetic instruction to the first four of a group of seven churches in Asia Minor. The church in Ephesus is the first to receive a message—maybe because of its well-known geographical priority as the best port of entry to the whole of Asia Minor, or perhaps because Ephesus had played a leading role in the beginnings of the Christian Church in the Gentile world. This church is commended for good, hard work and perseverance in doctrinal truth (v. 2), yet it is accused of losing its first love (v. 4). It can be so easy for us also to 'do' the right things and 'believe' the right things but for our hearts to have gone cold and our motivation to be wrong. Positively, though, this church hates the behaviour of a group called the Nicolaitans—a group which, although many scholars have identified it as gnostic, is not mentioned in any of the gnostic writings. Perhaps, as Irenaeus suggests, the group was formed by the deacon Nicolaus of Antioch (Acts 6:5) and simply rejected the apostolic decree to avoid food offered to idols (Acts 15).

Smyrna is next to be addressed. This church is commended for faithfully enduring suffering but is warned to brace itself: greater suffering is yet to come. However, the angel says, 'Do not fear what you are about to suffer' (v. 10). Why? Because their lives and future are in the hands of the one who has already experienced suffering, 'who was dead' yet 'came to life' (v. 8). He presently shares in and walks with them in their suffering (compare 1:9—20). Take comfort: although suffering will surely come to us all, we do not walk through it alone.

3 Hear what the Spirit says

Revelation 2:12—3:22

We continue our walk through the churches in Asia Minor. Pergamum is commended for persevering through suffering, yet condemned for permissively allowing idolatry to creep in. This city was the first in Asia to build a temple to a Roman emperor. The city's emblem was an image of Aesclepius, the serpent god of healing. The surrounding hills had many temples with throne-like altars dedicated to various gods. No wonder John saw 'Satan's throne' there (2:13).

The church in Thyatira had persevered through suffering but had allowed idolatry, mixed in with sexual immorality, to infect it. This mixture was characteristic of the pagan worship of the time. The church had been led astray by a false prophetess who, in many ways, reminded John of Jezebel in the Old Testament. When we read of how violent and idolatrous Jezebel was (1 Kings 16—21), it's no wonder that John calls those who have tolerated such a woman to repent.

In the late first century, Sardis was living off the reputation of a past but now faded glory. It was one of the oldest cities in Asia Minor but, even before it was nearly destroyed in the great earthquake of AD17, decline had already set in. The same was true of its church, which had 'a name of being alive' but was really 'dead' (3:1).

There is no accusation of sin and no warning of judgment to come in the message to Philadelphia, since this church is regarded as faithful (vv. 8b, 10a). The believers have discovered the 'key' principles of faithfulness and holiness; therefore, 'an open door' is set before them (v. 8). This church's solid faithfulness contrasts strongly with the tremors that had shaken the city some 80 years earlier.

Laodicea is in the worst condition of all the churches in the letters, and is the only church not commended for any good work. The metaphor of hot, cold and lukewarm water is unique to the city of Laodicea in the first century. Hierapolis was known for its medicinal hot water, Colossae was known for its pure, life-giving cold water, but Laodicea was known for its tepid, vomit-inducing, lukewarm water. You can still see the ruins of an aqueduct that piped calcium-rich water from a hot mineral spring five miles to the south, which slowly cooled to an emetic temperature. The conduct of this city's church is having the same effect on Christ as the water is having on the citizens!

The general message to these churches remains relevant today. Christ still commends us when we do good works. He still praises us when we persevere through suffering, and he still warns us to repent or face judgment when the pressures of the world in which we live cause us to compromise.

4 I will show you what must take place

Revelation 4—5

Many commentators claim that 4:1, '… what must take place after this', is the key to understanding the timing of the whole book. The question remains, however, as to which hermeneutical approach (that is, method of interpretation) we should use.

Preterists believe that almost all of Revelation now belongs in the past. When John wrote down his vision, the first three chapters described current events. Chapters 4:1—19:15 were, at the time, future events, but they were all fulfilled in the course of the first 400 years of the Christian Church. Only chapters 21—22 still remain to be fulfilled in the distant future.

Futurists believe that almost all of Revelation belongs in the future. Like the preterists, they believe that the first three chapters describe the contemporary churches of John's day, but they project all of the rest (4:1—22:21) into the distant future.

Historicists read the book of Revelation as a timetable of world history stretching from the time of the prophet John to the end of the world. According to this view, the present is punctuated by prophetic fulfilment.

The wise reader can look into this prophetic road map and discern which events happened yesterday, which events are happening today and which events might happen tomorrow. This approach allows the reader to find the exact verse that shows (in their interpretation) exactly where they stand in world history.

Idealists suggest that the meaning of the text is not confined to any historical time period but contains timeless spiritual truths that are relevant to all people at all times.

There is a bigger picture here, regardless of which approach we take. John is showing us a vision of the worship in heaven, not just as something for us to look forward to in the distant future but as a blueprint for our worship today. 'Holy, holy, holy,' the living creatures cry (4:8). They give 'glory and honour and thanks' to God (v. 9). They cry, 'Worthy is the Lamb' (5:12), and they fall down and worship (v. 14). Chapters 4 and 5 may tell us that the heavens resound with songs of praise to God, but chapters 2 and 3 tell us that this was not true on earth. Jesus prayed, 'Your will be done, on earth as it is in heaven' (Matthew 6:10), so what are we waiting for? When we enter the presence of Jesus, it doesn't matter if we are a preterist, futurist, historicist or idealist. As Charles Wesley sang, 'Let earth and heaven combine, angels and men agree, to praise in songs divine': the point is to join in with the worship.

5 Who can stand?

Revelation 6

Today we get on to some of the more mysteriously imaginative images in the book of Revelation. The 'four horsemen of the apocalypse' have exerted a fascination over writers, artists and musicians for centuries. On one level, their meaning depends on which hermeneutical model we use (see yesterday's notes), but there are some general principles here too. The sequence of the white horse (conquest), the red horse (civil unrest and persecution), the black horse (famine), and the pale horse (death) echoes the sequence of problems experienced by the seven churches in chapters 2—3. Those churches had first-hand experience of conquest, civil unrest, persecution, famine and death.

Leaving aside the live debate as to the identity of the rider on the white horse (there is an impasse here between those who identify this figure as the Christ who appears in Revelation 19 and those who identify him as an imitation or pseudo-Christ), we note that, at the very start of the chapter, the riders and their horses come only at the command of Jesus, the Lamb (v. 1). It is Christ who opens each seal to release them (vv. 3, 5, 7). Christ is in ultimate control, even of conquerors, persecution, famine and death. The suffering Christians in chapters 2—3 must surely have struggled to believe that Christ was ultimately sovereign over their disastrous circumstances. Yet here John reminds us that, as for Job, evil forces are only ever allowed to inflict trials on God's people with divine permission. Why? Revelation 6:1–8 shows us that trials come in order to purify us, punish us and prepare us. The central message of this chapter is that Christ rules over a chaotic world, and suffering does not occur by chance.

This 'revelation' (note the lower-case 'r' used here) is what inspired James to write, 'Consider it pure joy… whenever you face trials of many kinds, because you know that the testing of your faith develops perseverance… so that you may be mature and complete, not lacking anything' (James 1:2–4, NIV). So although the images here are perhaps the stuff of nightmares, the meaning they convey is one of comfort and reassurance to anyone who suffers.

6 God shall wipe away your tears

Revelation 7

Chapter 7 attempts to answer the question that chapter 6 ended with: 'Who can stand' on the 'great day of wrath'? (6:17). The first half of the chapter (vv. 1–8) explains how believers are 'sealed' so that they can persevere through the four trials of conquest, persecution, famine and death as described in chapter 6. The second half (vv. 9–17) shows us the heavenly reward offered to those who have made it through the suffering without losing their faith. But what does it mean to be 'sealed'?

The 'seal' may be interpreted in the light of the Passover/exodus story (Exodus 12:7, 13, 22–28), in which the blood of a slaughtered lamb was placed as a seal on the doorframe to protect God's people from the angel of death. The seal can also be interpreted in the light of Ezekiel 9:4–6, where the angel of the Lord 'marks' the faithful believers to protect them from destruction. Here the Hebrew word for 'mark' is *taw* (the full spelling of the last letter of the Hebrew alphabet, which, during the Babylonian captivity, was symbolised as † rather than T). John prophetically reinterprets these two Old Testament events to say that it is the blood of the Lamb of God and his cross that keep God's servants safe from suffering. While some interpreters take the 144,000 of God's servants in verses 3–8 as a literal number, most interpreters take it to be metaphorical, since all other numbers in the book are used in a metaphorical way. In this sense, the number represents the complete or perfect number of God's people.

The 'great multitude that no one could count' (v. 9) are dressed in white robes. Here John, standing last in a long line of prophets, draws heavily on a rich vein of Old Testament imagery. Cleansing dirty clothing symbolises the forgiveness of sins (see, for example, Isaiah 1:18; 64:6; Zechariah 3:3–5). But note the irony here: the saints make their robes 'white in the blood of the Lamb' (v. 14). The irony is that blood on white clothing is a stain that no amount of washing can remove! It is Christ's blood, not our own, that cleanses the stain of sin, and it is his death and suffering that bring us through our own times of suffering.

Guidelines

In our readings this week we have seen how seven historical churches at the end of the first century AD responded to suffering and trial. Pergamum challenges us to ask: what idols do we bow to today? An idol can be anything that takes first place in our heart before God. The message to Thyatira challenges each one of us to a renewed call to holiness and integrity. Sardis reminds us that we cannot live a vibrant and energetic Christian life relying only on past experiences. Every day we need a fresh touch from God to stop spiritual rigor mortis setting in. Philadelphia reminds us that the 'key' principles of faithfulness and holiness still remain 'key' for us today if we are to see doors open in our lives and our ministries.

What about us? What about the churches to which we belong? How do we respond to suffering and difficult times? What good works could we be commended for? Have we remained faithful? Which church do we most identify with? Christ still walks among the candlesticks (1:13). He walks among us. He commends us when we have done good works. He commends us when we have remained faithful to him, and he calls us to repent when either idolatry (anything that takes first place in our hearts before God) or immorality (anything that compromises our integrity and call to holiness) gets in the way of our being the people and church he has called us to be. The sovereign Lord allows suffering to come to purify us, to prepare us and even occasionally to punish us, so that we may stand before his throne dressed in white robes and sing the song of the redeemed: 'Salvation belongs to our God who is seated on the throne, and to the Lamb' (7:10).

1 The seventh seal

Revelation 8:1–6

Ingmar Bergman's iconic film *The Seventh Seal* (1957) tells the story of a medieval knight playing a game of chess with Death during the 14th-century pandemic of bubonic plague. Bergman named the film after the 'silence in heaven' (v. 1), as he struggled to understand how a loving God could remain silent while so many people suffered. The content of the seventh seal is mysteriously intriguing, for when the Lamb opens up this seal, there is 'silence in heaven for about half an hour'. What does this silence mean? Does it indicate a cessation of heavenly worship? Surely the rest of this book shows us that the worship of heaven is unceasing. Does the silence mean that the seal is empty and devoid of content? Surely that would indicate that the seal has sealed nothing, and a seal must seal something. So maybe the trumpets and bowls that follow are the actual content of the seventh seal? This view works on the 'recapitulation' theory, in which some argue that the seals are the trumpets and are the bowls: that is, the same cycle of seven events is told three times using three different metaphors.

This, of course, is a matter of interpretation. When I think of the number seven, I instantly think back to the creation story in Genesis. Just as the first revelation of God's dealings with humankind involved six successive days of creating followed by a well-earned rest, here the last revelation of God's dealings with humankind involves six days of unpicking or decreating followed by a well-earned rest. Here, then, the silence indicates God's rest. It is the final sabbath.

Whatever the seals mean within their specific social, historical and cultural context, today the seventh seal reminds us of two things. The first is that rest is important. Just as the earlier chapters show a blueprint for heavenly worship that we should emulate on earth, the seventh seal shows us the importance of taking a regular sabbath rest or holiday (literally 'holy-day'), especially to strengthen us for the challenge of suffering and difficulties that each one of us faces. The second thing is that although, when we suffer, it may seem to us (as it did to Bergman) that heaven is silent, this book reminds us that ultimately Christ is in control and working 'all things… together for good' (Romans 8:28) within his unfolding sovereign plan.

2 A warning against hardheartedness

Revelation 8:7—9:21

There is much to puzzle and confuse us in the book of Revelation. Saint Jerome is believed to have said that it contains 'as many riddles as it does words'. The Protestant Reformer Martin Luther is often credited with saying that it 'either finds a man mad or leaves him so'. Chapters 8 and 9 do not fail to puzzle or confuse!

Here we have seven angels blowing seven trumpets. Rather than trying to interpret what each trumpet represents in isolation, it is helpful to see what they represent in totality. The sounding of the first trumpet brings hail, fire and blood. The second turns the sea into blood. The third turns the water bitter. The fourth turns the sun, moon and stars dark. Chapter 9 starts with the blowing of the fifth trumpet, which signals the opening of the bottomless pit and the release of locust-scorpion-horse-human-lion chimeras; it then moves on to the sixth trumpet, which releases four angels to kill a third of humankind. The seventh angel/trumpet is reserved for chapter 11.

Since the times of Irenaeus and the Church Fathers, these trumpets have been interpreted in the light of the plagues inflicted upon the Egyptians before Israel's exodus (Exodus 7—11). So whereas Genesis provided the key to interpreting the seals, Exodus provides the key to interpreting the trumpets. It's worth noting here the purpose of the Exodus plagues. From the start of the story, we see that Pharaoh was never going to listen and repent (Exodus 4:21; 7:3–4). The plagues were sent to demonstrate that he was being judged because of the hardness of his heart. The same warning is found here. Regardless of how we interpret the trumpets, these chapters call each of us to take a silent half hour to examine our hearts and see if they have become hardened like Pharaoh's. We can suffer a kind of empathy fatigue and grow hardened to the needs of the homeless and downtrodden on our street, hardened to the suffering we see throughout the world on the news, hardened to the needs of our family, friends and those with whom we work and minister. Let us keep in mind that soon we will arrive at Revelation 21: the new creation, where suffering will be no more, is just around the corner. For now, though, let us continue to be tender-hearted towards the needy around us.

3 Sweet and sour scroll

Revelation 10

There is a wonderful scene in Roald Dahl's *Charlie and the Chocolate Factory* (1964). Wonka has come up with his greatest idea yet—the 'three-course dinner chewing gum'. This experimental candy starts by tasting like tomato soup, then develops into roast beef and baked potato flavour, before ending up tasting like blueberry pie and ice cream. The problem is, as Violet Beauregard soon discovers, that once the gum turns sweet, the chewer is turned into a giant blueberry!

The 'little scroll' that John is commanded to eat is equally remarkable. This scroll begins by tasting as sweet as honey but soon turns sour in the mouth. The scene is highly reminiscent of the commissioning of the prophet Ezekiel. We read that Ezekiel was told to eat a scroll that tasted 'as sweet as honey' (Ezekiel 3:3), but had 'words of lament and mourning and woe' written on it (2:10). For both John and Ezekiel, the joy of being commissioned as a prophet is but a brief and fleeting pleasure in the face of the seriousness of the content of the message.

The message is that 'the mystery of God will be accomplished, just as he announced to his servants the prophets' (v. 7). The 'gospel' or 'good news' of Christ, including both the sweet flavour of salvation and the sour flavour of judgment, was prophetically 'announced' by God to the prophets throughout the Old Testament. This is why Jesus could say that all of the Law and Prophets found their fulfilment in him (see, for example, Matthew 5:17). Yet the future dimension of the good news that 'will be accomplished' reminds us of the 'now but not quite yet' dimension of our salvation. On the one hand we are saved, but on the other hand we are *being* saved. We are all called to be messengers of the good news of Jesus. It is a great joy indeed to see a person respond to the wonderful revelation of the love of God expressed in the death and resurrection of Jesus, but sometimes God calls us to bring 'sour' and 'bitter' tasting words to individuals and societies. The task of speaking out against sin, corruption and injustice is not so instantly gratifying, yet it is important none the less.

4 The two witnesses

Revelation 11

John Wesley noted that the book of Revelation 'was given to a banished man; and men in affliction understand and relish it most'. Our own suffering and affliction not only turn us to seek answers in this book but may also actually help us to understand the meaning of the book itself. Whereas the first six trumpets focused on the judgments upon those who reject Christ through hardheartedness, this chapter shows us the relationship between godless unbelievers and godly believers. The godless persecute the godly. It has always been so and always will be.

In this chapter we read of the affliction of the two witnesses. The Greek word for 'witnesses' in verse 3 is *martusin* and the Greek word for 'testimony' in verse 7 is *marturian*. From these words comes the modern English word 'martyr', meaning one who dies for his or her religious beliefs. There is a gentle irony in the way the witnesses or martyrs attain their victory: it is won in the same paradoxical way that Christ achieved his victory through dying on the cross. Through suffering and death, true life is attained.

Who are these two witnesses? Do they represent two concepts like 'the word of God' and 'the testimony of Jesus', or the Old and New Testaments? Are they two individual and resurrected prophets—for example, Moses and Elijah, or Paul and Peter? Elijah's prayers shut up the heavens for 42 months so that it did not rain (compare 1 Kings 18:1; Luke 4:25 and James 5:17 with the time periods given in verses 2–3 and the 'power to shut up the sky' in verse 6). But note that even John the Baptist wasn't the literally resurrected Elijah. He came only 'in the spirit and power of Elijah' (Luke 1:17), yet his words are described as being like a 'lamp that burned and gave light' (compare John 5:35 with Revelation 11:4). So the two witnesses here have the prophetic mantle of the prophets but are not literally those prophets resurrected.

The prophet Joel had foretold that the entire community of believers would receive the gift of prophecy (Joel 2:28–32), and the early church believed that Joel's prophecy began its fulfilment on the day of Pentecost (Acts 2:17–21). The whole Church is called to be a prophetic witness to the world in every age. In that sense, the answer to the question 'Who are the witnesses?' is 'You are!' (see Acts 1:8).

5 The woman clothed with the sun

Revelation 12

The mysteriously intriguing images that give Revelation such a fascination for its readers continue in chapter 12 with a vision of 'a woman clothed with the sun, with the moon under her feet, and on her head a crown of twelve stars' (v. 1). Who is this woman? Does she represent Eve, who, in pain, would bring forth a child to crush the serpent's head (Genesis 3:15–17)? Does she represent Jacob, Rachel and the twelve tribes of Israel (Genesis 37:9), or Abraham, Sarah and their offspring as numerous as the stars (15:5–6)? Does she represent the nation of Israel—frequently described in scripture as either a faithful or unfaithful wife or virgin? Is she a metaphor for the city of Jerusalem (Song of Songs 6:4, 10)? John would have been familiar with all of this Old Testament imagery, and gathers it all together to form a rich image of the entire community of faithful believers, both before and after Christ, who are persecuted for their faith.

The great red dragon is the devil himself, who persecutes godly and faithful believers and, indeed, attempts both to tempt the Messiah and to kill him throughout his life and ministry (see Luke 4:1–12, 28–30). Although it appeared that the dragon had 'devoured' the Messiah at the cross, through the resurrection the Messiah was 'caught up to God' and the dragon failed. The woman (the metaphor for faithful believers) flees into the wilderness to a place prepared for her by God—a place where she will be nourished. Here, again, our minds are drawn back to the exodus from Egypt and the time of sojourn in the desert as God's chosen people awaited their entry into the promised land. They were nourished there with manna, the bread of heaven (Exodus 16). When Jesus the Messiah spent 40 days in the wilderness and was tempted by the great red dragon, he said, 'Man does not live by bread alone, but on every word that comes from the mouth of God' (Matthew 4:4). We too may find ourselves in a desert, in a wilderness. It is a paradoxical place where, in the midst of persecution, we can find divine protection. In the face of temptation we can find spiritual nourishment. When life feels like a dry wilderness, may you feed on the word of God until you reach the promised land.

6 The two beasts

Revelation 13—14

Of all the images in the Apocalypse, the two agents of the great red dragon described in chapter 13 have intrigued and terrified, in equal extent, more than any other image in scripture. The beast from the sea (vv. 1–10) is indescribably terrible and horrendous. The beast from the earth (vv. 11–18) is harmless in appearance, and all the more deadly for that very reason. Throughout history, many interpreters have believed they have seen the beasts arise in their own day in various shapes and forms, but history has invariably proven such interpretations wrong. For this reason, a general rather than specific interpretation is helpful.

The beast from the sea represents the hand of the dragon—the power of Satan working in and through the political and governmental systems of the world in every age to persecute and oppress those who have faith in Jesus. The beast from the land represents the mind of the dragon—the power of Satan working in and through empty religion, ideologies and philosophies in every age to deceive and confuse those who have faith in Jesus. It's tempting to focus exclusively on these fearsome and fantastical images, but, if we do so, we forget the centrality of the heavenly messenger with 'the eternal gospel to proclaim' (14:6)—the good news that Christ has died and is risen, death is beaten and eternal life is the inheritance of all who believe. The proclamation of this good news is now our responsibility and privilege (Matthew 28:19–20) and should always occupy more of our time and effort than trying to decode strange Hebrew puzzles such as the number 666.

Chapter 14 is full of the language of worship. Mount Zion is used throughout the Old Testament as a symbol of God's dwelling place. The playing of harps, the singing of a new song, and the throne (vv. 1–4) all allude to worship. The cloud symbolises God's glory and the golden crown his kingship; the temple and the altar further point us to worship (vv. 14–15). Why does John bring us back to such a scene of heavenly worship here? Because when we feel as if the beasts of this age are oppressing, persecuting, deceiving and confusing us, we should remember that the Lamb is on his throne. He is the glorious true king and we are his redeemed people. As we worship him, we will rise above those troubles.

Guidelines

Try googling a phrase like 'apocalyptic image' or 'apocalyptic art' and you will find millions of hits portraying horror, terror, cataclysm, death and destruction. Yet, if this week's readings have taught us anything, it is that through such richly fantastical imagery comes the central message that the Lamb is on his throne, that he is in control of this world's future, and that in the midst of persecution and affliction we can find hope and comfort. We have learnt that rest and silence are divinely sanctioned principles and important in helping us face difficulties. We have learnt that just because God seems silent while people suffer, it doesn't mean that he doesn't care. Of course he cares! If Revelation tells us anything, it tells us that all those who suffer righteously will be eternally comforted, and all those who persecute the righteous will be eternally punished.

We have received a warning against hardheartedness and have been called not to let emotional fatigue set in when faced with the needs around us. We have been challenged to speak out against injustice and oppression—even when the words taste unpalatable—for we are all called to be prophets and witnesses. We have seen how the ironic victory of the Lamb and his saints lies in apparent defeat, and from this we should take comfort that when we feel broken and defeated, we share in the paradoxical victory of the cross. When life feels dry and barren, we can feed on living bread. And when the beasts of this age oppress, persecute, deceive and confuse us, our worship of the Lamb, with the new song he has placed on our lips, has the ability to lift us into the presence of the throne room of God.

Who ever said that Revelation was only about horror, terror, cataclysm, death and destruction?

1 The heavenly tabernacle

Revelation 15—16

Chapter 15 begins with a vision of heavenly temple worship. Again John draws richly from the Hebrew scriptures with which he was so well acquainted. The 'tent of witness' (v. 5) is the heavenly version of the Old Testament tabernacle—the symbol of God's presence among his people as they journeyed through the wilderness after the exodus (Exodus 40:34–38). The 'testimony' or 'witness' here refers to the Ten Commandments, which God gave to Moses at Mount Sinai (Exodus 20). Moses placed the Ten Commandments in the ark of the tabernacle to show that God's word was in the midst of his people (Exodus 16:34; 25:8), and that he would continue to reveal his will to his people (25:21–22; see Acts 7:44). This moral and legal framework was not to be seen as enslaving or binding, but as God's great gift of 'word' and 'will' to the world. The tabernacle and the ark also represented the mercy of God. This was the place where sacrifices were offered to atone for the sins of the people and nation (Leviticus 16:14).

The seven bowls of chapter 16 are a repetition or recapitulation of the seven trumpets (see notes on 8:1–6). The plagues strike in the same order: the first trumpet/bowl strikes the earth; the second trumpet/bowl strikes the sea; the third trumpet/bowl strikes the rivers; the fourth trumpet/bowl strikes the sun; the fifth trumpet/bowl strikes the realm of the wicked; the sixth trumpet/bowl strikes the Euphrates; and the seventh trumpet/bowl strikes the world with final judgment.

The Exodus plagues provided the model for both cycles, but Leviticus provides the background to the way the plagues strike. The seven angels are commanded to 'pour out the seven bowls' (16:1). Remember that chapter 15 is happening in the heavenly version of the tabernacle, so the 'pouring out' reminds us of the sacrificial blood 'poured out' by the priest at the base of the altar and in front of the sanctuary to cleanse the tabernacle and people from sin (Leviticus 4:6–7, 17–18; 8:15). Here in Revelation the 'pouring out' of the bowls is a priestly act to cleanse the earth from the defilement of sin.

As we saw in chapter 10, all of this Old Testament imagery found its fulfilment in Jesus. He fulfilled and perfected the Law, and he himself became both high priest and substitutionary sacrifice to atone for our sins.

2 'Come out of her'

Revelation 17—18

Revelation 17 and 18 focus on the fall and destruction of Babylon the Great. She is a fascinating, mysterious, bloodthirsty and dangerously seductive character, but who is she? As we have seen, John was steeped in the language and imagery of the Old Testament. He would have been familiar with Genesis 11 and the story of the tower of Babel—a picture of human rejection of the rule of God, rebellion against the divine will, and spiritual confusion (the Hebrew word for Babel literally means 'confusion'). John would also have found in the Old Testament a picture of a nation at war with Israel who eventually destroyed the temple and led God's people into physical captivity and religious infidelity.

John draws richly on this imagery here to refer, within his own social and historical context, to Imperial Rome—the city that destroyed the second temple in AD70 and persecuted the early church. Throughout the history of the Church, commentators have believed that they have seen Babylon arise in their own times. In the first 400 years after the birth of Christ, 'Babylon' was generally used as a cryptogram or code word for the city of Rome and the empire. From the time of Augustine through to the early medieval period, Babylon generally symbolised the seductive influence of the world on the church. During the Reformation, Babylon was frequently identified as papal Rome or the pope in Rome. In more modern times, Babylon has been identified as anyone or anything ranging from previous prime ministers of Great Britain and the police force, through to the cities of London, Los Angeles and New York and even the US Treasury Department.

Regardless of how we specifically interpret this symbol of economic and religious oppression, the centrality of the call to believers to 'come out of her' remains the same (18:4). Babylon as a symbol of economic oppression and religious corruption retains her relevance today when we consider the great economic and financial crisis that began in 2007 and is continuing as I write. Babylon warns us of the bloodthirsty nature of unbridled financial greed and of the destructive effect that unregulated financial markets can have on innocent people. Babylon also warns us of the crisis of belief occurring in our postmodern society, which attempts to relativise the truth of the gospel. The call to 'come out of' and reject these Babylons needs to be heard today.

3 A wedding invitation

Revelation 19

In this chapter we are invited to the marriage feast of the Lamb—and we are the Bride! The marriage metaphor symbolises a close, loving and intimate relationship between God and his people. But how has the bride—the Church—made herself ready? By faithfully persevering through suffering, by passing through the fire of Babylon's economic and religious persecution, and by doing good and righteous deeds. Ultimately, though, the Church is made ready because of what God has done through Christ on our behalf. The Lamb did for us what we could never do for ourselves.

We will stand at the marriage feast in pure garments because we have been made righteous, justified and vindicated by the cross of Jesus. As Paul writes in Ephesians 5:25–27, it is Christ alone who sanctifies and purifies the Church so that at the end of time she will be presented to him as a 'holy and blameless' bride.

Verses 11–21 describe Christ's defeat and judgment of the ungodly powers that persecute and afflict believers throughout the ages. Here Christ is given four titles. The first is 'Faithful and True' (v. 11), a development of the name 'faithful and true witness' given to Christ in Revelation 3:14, which reminds us that this is the same Jesus who walks amid his church as she is suffering.

A further title of Christ is 'Word of God' (v. 13), which is also symbolised by the sword in his mouth—the actual weapon of judgment used to overcome the forces of evil (vv. 13, 15, 21). It is with the same word of God that we are to overcome the enemy in our own day (Ephesians 6:17).

Another title is known by no one other than himself (v. 12). In the Old Testament, to know a name means to have control over the one named. The secrecy of this third name refers to Christ's absolute sovereignty over humankind's understanding of his true nature. Some people have the revelation of his name and, therefore, can know him as Saviour, but to others the name is revealed only at the last judgment. This links in with the last name: 'King of Kings and Lord of Lords' (v. 16). This is a revelation that we, as believers, may confess today, but one day even those who do not believe will have to bow the knee and confess that Jesus is Lord (Philippians 2:9–11).

4 Are you pre, post or pan?

Revelation 20

Whenever anyone gets into a debate about the book of Revelation, you can guarantee that it won't be long before the meaning of the millennium, or 1000-year rule of Christ, is discussed. Chapter 20 is central to this debate. Generally there are three main stances one may take. Premillennialists believe that Christ will return before (pre) the start of the millennium; then Christ will rule with the Church on earth for 1000 years. Postmillennialists believe that Christ will return after (post) the millennium. There will be a 1000-year golden age when the Church will rule on earth before Christ's return, and this period will end with Christ's second coming. Amillennialists do not believe that the millennium is a literal 1000 years but believe that the millennium started at Christ's resurrection with the binding of Satan, and will conclude at his second coming.

Premillennialists often take an over-pessimistic view of world history, seeing the world as getting progressively worse. Postmillennialists often take an over-optimistic view of world history, seeing the world as getting progressively better. Amillennialists usually take a more symbolic view of Revelation as the timeless and continual struggle between the forces of good and evil, in which good will ultimately triumph over evil.

The stance we take on the millennium is, at the end of the day, a question of hermeneutics. It is up to each one of us to decide for ourselves. Yet, if we consider the morally instructive dimension of prophecy expressed by John throughout his vision—that those who continue in good works and endure faithfully through suffering will receive the blessing of eternal life—and we interpret this passage in the light of other scripture (for example, 'No one knows about that day...' in Matthew 24:36, or the parable of the wise and foolish virgins in Matthew 25:1–13), then we hear John calling us to move beyond trying merely to discern when the millennium will be inaugurated. His revelation challenges us to live today and every day in the reality of the imminent return of Christ. Christ could return tonight, and John wants us to be ready.

By the way, the 'pan' in the title of today's reading refers to a terrible old joke a friend of mine told me when asked if he was a pre- or post-millennialist. His answer: 'I'm *pan*-millennial: it'll all pan out in the end!'

5 New for old

Revelation 21

Chapter 21 begins with a vision of 'a new heaven and a new earth' (v. 1). Here the word 'new' (*kainos*) refers to the quality of this creation rather than the chronology or timing of the arrival of this creation. The 'new' heaven and earth will be a permanent and perfect creation compared with our impermanent and imperfect creation. The 'new' creation follows the pattern of Christ's death and resurrection, and the resurrection that Christ's new life guarantees to us. Paul's teaching on the resurrection in 1 Corinthians can be applied here: just as the old body is perishable, the old creation is perishable; just as the new body is imperishable, the new creation is imperishable (1 Corinthians 15:42–45). We read in Revelation 21:4 that all those things that typify the fall of humanity into sin—the pain, suffering and death that entered the world in the first Eden—will be removed in the last Eden. This new creation will be just as God had always intended the first one to be.

Why are the measurements of the new city included? It wouldn't be in keeping with the figurative nature of other numbers in this book to interpret these dimensions literally: some scholars have tried to do this and concluded that such a city would be architecturally unusual. Rather, the city is explicitly identified as a metaphorical symbol of the whole body of the Church, Christ's bride (v. 9). Therefore, the measuring of the city and its parts is a picture of God's intimate knowledge of and interest in the very smallest details of his people, and guarantees the security and protection of its inhabitants against all harm. These 'new' walls will provide eternal protection, in contrast to old Jerusalem's walls, which were broken down by God's enemies.

The twelve jewels adorning the foundation stones of the wall (v. 19) are the same as those found on the high priest's breastplate in Exodus 28:17–20 and 39:8–14. This suggests that the very stones of this place are priestly. Here, as in other places in scripture, stones represent 'precious' people. In verse 22 John says, 'I saw no temple…' So in which temple will these priestly people serve? Actually, though, John did see the temple— just not a physically built temple. Throughout Revelation, John has repeatedly seen 'the Lord God' and 'the Lamb'. They personally are the temple.

6 Holy, holy, holy, holy, holy

Revelation 22

When God created this world, everything he made was 'very good' (Genesis 1:31), yet we are slowly destroying it. God created the waters to be crystal clear, yet we've choked them with oil slicks. God created the trees to heal the nations—removing carbon dioxide and reoxygenating the air—yet we're responsible for deforestation on a vast scale. This is clearly not what God intended for his world.

The final chapter of Revelation is a hope-filled antidote to a world in crisis. It starts with a wonderful scene of a future fertile land, with a river of crystal clear water and a tree whose leaves have healing properties. It is Eden recreated—the paradise in which God always intended humans to live. We see the 'river of the water of life' (v. 1). Elsewhere John uses this imagery to symbolise the Holy Spirit (John 7:37–39; see also John 3:5; 4:10–24; 1 John 5:7–8). So here, in this river, we see the Spirit, the 'giver of life', flowing out from both the Father (the throne of God) and the Son (the Lamb), bringing life to the people of God. We also see the 'tree of life'. Eating the healing fruit of this tree undoes the effects of eating the fruit of 'the tree of the knowledge of good and evil' (Genesis 2:17), which brought sin, suffering and death into the world.

The rest of the chapter (vv. 6–21) shows us the prophetically instructive and moral purpose of the book as a call to God's people to remain holy even through persecution and suffering. John closes his revelation by calling us to holiness five times, through either the promise of a blessing for living a holy life or a warning of judgment for living an unholy life. The first call to holiness is in verse 7: 'Keep the words'. John is saying, 'Do what I told you!" The second call is in verse 9—again 'Keep the words' or 'Do what I told you!' The third call to holiness is in verses 11–12: 'Don't do evil.' The fourth call is in verses 14–15: 'Wash your robes', and the fifth and final call to holiness is in verses 18–19, where John again challenges his readers to obey the words of this book. Can't you just hear John shouting down through the ages, 'Do you get my point? God has called you to live a holy life… so do it!'

Guidelines

Back in the 1980s the rock band REM sang, 'It's the end of the world as we know it… and I feel fine!' What a great way of summing up John's purpose in writing! You see, for those who belong to the Lamb, the terrifying imagery in this book shouldn't be a source of fear or worry but a source of comfort. If, over the past three weeks, John has been saying anything, he has been urging us to take comfort in the fact that although we may suffer in the present, and although it may seem as if the devil has the upper hand in the present, in reality the Lamb is on his throne, victorious over suffering, pain, death and the devil. Although we may not see this with our own eyes right now, it is true none the less. We see that the church of John's day had the same problems and issues as the church of our own day—so take comfort. We see that the beasts and the Babylons of our own day will eventually be destroyed—so take comfort. Regardless of how we interpret the individual images such as seals, trumpets and bowls, in the end all things will be made new—so take comfort. Above all, live your lives under the imminent hope that that day could be today!

FURTHER READING

D. Aune, *Revelation* (Word Biblical Commentary Series) (Nelson, 1997–98).

G.K. Beale, *The Book of Revelation* (New International Greek Testament Commentary Series) (Paternoster, 1999).

A.Y. Collins, *The Apocalypse (Revelation)* (The New Jerome Biblical Commentary, 2nd edn) (Geoffrey Chapman, 1996).

J. Massyngberde Ford, *Revelation: A New Translation with Introduction and Commentary* (The Anchor Bible Series) (Doubleday, 1975).

Habakkuk

Habakkuk, despite his strange name (unusual even in the Old Testament), is one of the few prophets with whom we sense an immediate connection as he pours out his heart in passionate prayer. He lives, as we do, in a violent, insecure world, but God is silent, neither listening nor saving—and this is the God who has promised to hear and answer prayer. Wrestling with his agony, refusing to give up and slip into apathy, Habakkuk is truly for us a kindred spirit.

Habakkuk's horizons were inevitably narrower than today's. His known world was smaller than ours, where global events can be accessed in mere seconds: for us, the sights and sounds are little short of immediate. But Iraq was part of his problem, too. One great power of the day, the Assyrian empire, was crumbling, and a new power, Babylon (Iraq), was gaining ground. By 612BC, the Babylonians were in control. There was trouble nearer home, as well, in Judah itself. Law and order were breaking down. Where was God in all this?

By any standards, this book is great poetry, even in translation. Historically important, it gives a glimpse into ancient lives, depicting helpless individuals in a frightening world and powerful individuals governed by greed and brutality. As holy scripture, though, it is more than that. It is God's voice challenging us as we read today.

These notes are based mainly on the New Revised Standard Version of the Bible.

31 October–6 November

1 Unanswered prayer

Habakkuk 1:1–4

Habakkuk the prophet is a visionary: this is what he 'saw' (v. 1). In other words, he sees beyond the immediate to the deeper questions of relationship with God. This is a very personal book—it shows the prophet in his intimate dealings with God—but he voices, too, the distress and bewilderment of his people. Habakkuk's prayer is not self-centred. He longs for stability in his disintegrating society, for justice and right order to prevail, giving vent to his bitterness not in pious phrases but with blunt exasperation, even accusation: 'Lord, how long shall I cry… and you will not listen?' He piles up words (six different terms) for violence and strife. Even worse, the law (Torah) is ineffective ('paralysed': v. 4, NIV) and justice is, literally, 'twisted'. The prophet's bitterness is increased by the fact that it is God who shows him these things (v. 3)—God, who can right the wrongs suffered by the oppressed, if only he will take action. But where is his answer? Isn't this the prayer that we often pray as we witness erupting anger and unbelievable brutality between individuals and nations?

This is powerful poetry, still ringing true over many centuries. Acceptance of a remote, uncaring God eases some of the problems, though not the grief and heartache. But that is not our God, and nor was it Habakkuk's God. The prophet's bewilderment at unanswered prayer is intense, and so is ours, though we have the joy of knowing, through the cross, that when God seems most hidden he is most active and triumphant.

Habakkuk holds on. His faith is troubled but it holds fast. In his distress he brings his passionate complaint to that same silent, apparently inactive God. Israel's God is his only hope—of that Habakkuk is sure—so he remains in dialogue with God.

This is an honest book, with no pretence of piety and no deferential, pious language—just a straightforward encounter with God. Blunt and outspoken, Habakkuk's confidence shows that he is not afraid to confront the God with whom he is in personal relationship. In intimate dealings with God, he voices what others must have felt.

Where did Habakkuk find this confidence to wrestle so boldly with God? The answer must surely be in the constant practice of worship, exemplified in the Psalms. There the prophet would have heard the solemn pronouncement: 'Once God has spoken; twice have I heard this; that power belongs to God, and steadfast love belongs to you, O Lord' (Psalm 62:11–12).

2 The Lord of history

Habakkuk 1:5–11

The prophet in Israel had a dual role—of prayer and preaching. Habakkuk has wrestled with God in prayer; now he brings God's response, and a strange answer it seems at first. Injustice at home and the perversion of law had troubled him, but God tells him to look further afield: 'Look at the nations, and see!' (v. 5).

Faith always needs a broader vision, looking beyond the immediate problem to see that God is at work in the world, even in the turmoil of nations, unlikely though it may appear. For Isaiah, Assyria had been the instrument of God's judgment (Isaiah 10:5); later, Cyrus of Persia became God's agent of salvation (44:28). So now Habakkuk is challenged to see God in control even amid the terrifying might of the Chaldeans (v. 6). God's answer seems a strange kind of encouragement for the fragmented, unstable society on whose behalf the prophet has been pleading. Yet it affirms the truth we do well to remember, that God is sovereign and, although human minds often cannot fathom the mystery of his ways, God is love.

For us, the challenge to faith comes in an equally unstable world amid changing circumstances. 'Look... and see.' Does the church seem to be losing ground at home? Broaden your vision to the worldwide church, to those places where faithful Christians stand firm against persecution and, in their sacrifice and suffering, the seed of life is sown. Nearer home, where 'fresh expressions of church' bring new vitality to Christian witness, God is at work in our world, if only we have eyes to see.

In Habakkuk's dramatic picture of military success, with all its brutality ('they gather captives like sand', v. 9), we glimpse the seeds of ultimate failure (v. 7). Where, in their reckoning, is the God of justice? Where is the dignity of creation in God's likeness? The root of the trouble lies in the poem's last line (v. 11): 'their own might is their god.' Sadly, Israel, too, often failed, forgetting the Lord. And what of us?

This is dramatic, powerful poetry but it is more than that. The apostle Paul, preaching one sabbath in the synagogue at Antioch in Pisidia, quoted Habakkuk's words from the early Greek translation (the Septuagint) as he told of God's greater work in Jesus' resurrection, offering freedom and forgiveness for 'everyone who believes' (Acts 13:39–41). From the late seventh century BC, down through early Christian preaching, God's living, life-changing word challenges and encourages us today.

3 A troubled believer

Habakkuk 1:12–17

God has responded to Habakkuk's prayer, but still the questions come: 'Why? Oh, why?' And so the prophet challenges God again with question after question. Why is there an apparently unbridgeable gulf between faith and reality? Habakkuk is a believer, but a troubled one. He starts with expressions of worship: God is holy and eternal; God is a rock of protection; God is too pure to have contact with evil. Such are Habakkuk's premises. Yet how does God's inaction, his silence in the face of evil, reflect his nature? These are deep and troubling questions, to which Habakkuk must find an answer. The advance of the Babylonians seems as random as trawling for fish. Before their advancing armies, not only Israel but also other nations face destruction 'without mercy' (v. 17).

Habakkuk, the troubled believer, brings his doubts to the one who is still 'Lord my God, my Holy One' (v. 12). The relationship of faith holds, despite the puzzling doubts. Was faith easier in the ancient world than it is for us? Habakkuk's agonising cries give the answer, but he also shows us the way to deal with honest doubts. The Old Testament is never hesitant to question God and his ways. The psalmists are bold in their approach, and so, above all, is Job—an encouragement today to be honest about the awkward questions that test our faith. God is is, after all, the one 'to whom all hearts are open, all desires known, and from whom no secrets are hidden' (Prayer of Preparation, Holy Communion). When we agonise over the question of how faith and reality can coexist in this troubled world, let us lay hold on God, mindful, as Habakkuk was, that despite all the problems he is still 'my God', the one to whom I have committed myself. God does not confuse doubt with blasphemy. It was Job's anguished questions that God approved, not the conventional piety of his friends (Job 42:7). Jesus, too, in the extremity of distress, voiced a question: 'My God, my God, why have you forsaken me?' (Mark 15:34).

To close our eyes to problems, making God and his ways fit into our pre-conceived ideas and our too neat and tidy theology, is not faith but timid self-defence. It is, in short, self-deception.

Habakkuk's challenge to God ends with an unanswered question. How can he square what he sees in the world with his belief in a God of justice? Habakkuk must wait in patience. His journey from fear to faith has only just begun.

4 Waiting for God's answer

Habakkuk 2:1–5

The prophet's task was not easy. It took courage to challenge God, and patience to await his answer in God's good time. Habakkuk sees himself as a watchman on the city ramparts, alert day and night for signs of dan-ger or, in time of siege, for the first glimmer of hope (see Psalm 130:6). The message to be proclaimed was never at the prophet's disposal: it came in God's own time. Habakkuk was not the only prophet who had to learn this lesson. Jeremiah, at a moment of dramatic confrontation with Hananiah, a powerful adversary, when an immediate response seemed necessary, had to wait for an answer that came 'some time af-ter' (Jeremiah 28:10–12). It's not easy to wait with injustice rampant and danger threatening, but Habakkuk, too, is still 'watching to see...' (v. 1): again there is an emphasis on having open eyes. Though delayed, the answer will surely come, to be made clear for all to see, understand-able at a glance. Contrary to appearances, the future belongs not with pride or greed but with those who live faithfully ('by their faith', v. 4) in God's way. Faithfulness means long-term commitment and quiet confi-dence in God—a matter of faith, not sight.

A prophet's responsibility was heavy and inescapable. Ezekiel 33:7–9 spells it out: the messenger bears the people's guilt himself if he fails to give due warning, whether through cowardice or negligence. Prophecy re-quired confident trust in the reliability of the message and assurance that God was its author, whether a promise of salvation or a word of warning. As we study this often neglected book, let's remember that we are follow-ing in famous footsteps. Twice we find Paul quoting from Habakkuk, preaching on 1:5 about God's extraordinary actions in Christ's death and resurrection (see Acts 13:41), then drawing on 2:4 as the foundation of his argument in Romans 3:21–24 that faith is the ground of our commitment, shaping and empowering our entire life with God.

Waiting for the answer to our prayers, for God to fulfil his promises, is not easy. We pray, 'Your kingdom come, your will be done on earth', and still violence and greed surge around us. Where is his rule of peace and love? 'If it seems to tarry, wait for it; it will surely come' (v. 3). Patient waiting means active commitment to the kingdom, but its coming may not be quite as we expect.

5 Theft by fraud

Habakkuk 2:6–8

The rest of chapter 2 contains a series of five 'woes' against those who, for selfish advantage, burden others with grief. 'Woe to him…' (NIV) conveys the meaning more strongly than 'Alas…' (NRSV). This passage is not so much a lament over evil as a forthright declaration of God's commitment to overthrow injustice. Wherever injustice is found, it is an attack on the very foundation of God's kingdom and a denial of his nature. He is indeed 'Mighty King, lover of justice' (Psalm 99:4).

The first woe sounds uncannily modern to our ears: '[Woe to you] who heap up what is not your own! … Will not… those who make you tremble wake up?' (vv. 6–7). This is fraud on a grand scale, and fraud is theft. Here is the same concern for the weak and powerless that motivated Habakkuk's complaint to God in chapter 1. But justice for the oppressed means judgment on the oppressor. Some had amassed wealth from goods that were taken in pledge and never returned to their owners, in blatant defiance of Israelite law—a crime that Amos had earlier inveighed against (Amos 2:8; see Deuteronomy 24:12–13). The plunderer himself will be plundered, says the prophet, whether his wealth was gained through the unjust structures of society (v. 6: still a present danger) or extorted on a grander scale on the international scene (v. 8). Nations as well as individuals are accountable to the God of justice, the Old Testament reminds us.

The prophet has not yet finished his accusations against the avaricious.

They are guilty not only of human bloodshed but of violence against the earth itself. Such is the devastation caused by those who multiply their own wealth, whatever the cost, plundering earth's resources—a danger to which our society has recently awakened. Now the oceans, too, need protection, lest we store up unknown perils for future generations. More than two and a half millennia ago, the prophet glimpsed such dangers.

In the ancient words of Habakkuk we come close to the heart of the Christian gospel, with its concern for the disadvantaged and the outcast. God's ways are not ours; nor are the values of his kingdom those of the world. The gospel overturns the hierarchical structures of society, as the Magnificat proclaims: 'He has brought down the powerful from their thrones, and lifted up the lowly' (Luke 1:52). This is an ideal that still awaits fulfilment, when the kingdom comes for which Jesus taught his disciples to pray.

6 Individual and corporate greed

Habakkuk 2:9–14

Let those who thoughtlessly write off the Old Testament as out of date take note of these verses, striking in their modernity. Habakkuk doesn't mince matters: greed brings both disgrace and disaster. His words are remarkably similar to Jeremiah's condemnation of Judah's King Jehoiakim. The two prophets were virtually contemporary, and perhaps Habakkuk, too, had this tyrannical ruler in mind. Jeremiah had said, 'Woe to him who builds his house by unrighteousness, and his upper rooms by injustice; who makes his neighbour work for nothing' (Jeremiah 22:13). Habakkuk's words are less specific: not only rulers were at fault. The corruption went deeper.

We, today, are not exempt. Greed possesses our lives. The temptation to seek personal aggrandisement, finding status in impressive possessions, is still rife. Yet, says the prophet, ostentatious greed will not go unpunished. Its downfall will be heralded from the housetops (in the national press?) or, to use Habakkuk's graphic language, the very stones and woodwork will cry out against the monstrous injustice of affluence built on crushing the powerless (v. 11). What a contrast to Jesus' words as he rode triumphantly into Jerusalem on his journey to the cross! 'If these were silent,' he said of the excited crowd, 'the stones would shout out' (Luke 19:40).

A strong concern for social justice runs throughout the pages of the Old Testament. It was expressed not only by prophets like Amos, who told his hearers, in no uncertain terms, that worship without justice was empty ritual, unacceptable to God (Amos 5:21–24). The laws in Deuteronomy, too, emphasise concern for fellow humans and their animals (Deuteronomy 22:1–4, 8), another modern touch.

With the third woe (vv. 12–14), the prophet condemns a still more extensive evil: whole cities founded on violence and fraud. His thought moves between the guilt of individuals and the guilt of nations, primarily the Babylonians. Their evil was on a grander scale than Jehoiakim's (he was, after all, ruler of a tiny country), but it is the same in kind: they are 'brothers under the skin'. Yet the last word doesn't lie with earth's transient kingdoms, however grand. Nations still rise and fall. Even today we see power shifting from West to East. Habakkuk foresees a glorious future in which 'the earth will be filled with the knowledge of the glory of the Lord, as the waters cover the sea' (v. 14). Isaiah's portrayal of the coming Messiah expresses a similar hope (Isaiah 11:9), but Habakkuk's vision goes even beyond Isaiah's in his emphasis on 'the glory of the Lord.'

Guidelines

Habakkuk's role was twofold, involving prayer and preaching. In both he was direct and honest, uninhibited in approaching God and courageous in addressing the nation's ills. His ministry, like ours, meant patient waiting, accepting the tension between promise and fulfilment. Patient waiting is not the same as listless apathy or quiet indifference. It means active, long-term commitment to the kingdom. It means faith, not sight.

To what extent have the words of this ancient prophet both warned and encouraged us in our very different ministries?

1 Alcoholism and ecology

Habakkuk 2:15–17

Here is another surprise! Modern Britain's growing problem with alcohol abuse and the pressing urgency of ecological issues both find an echo in Habakkuk's ancient words. The perils of drunken behaviour, as well as the devastation of Lebanon's famous trees and its wild creatures, were of concern in what we tend to discount as 'primitive' times.

Habakkuk's poetry—in part literal, in part metaphorical—ranges widely, applying on the international scene to the rising Babylonian power and probably also, within Israel's own society, to its King Jehoiakim. The Babylonians, like the Assyrians before them, had plundered the land. So, too, had the notoriously extravagant Jehoiakim (reigning from 609 to 598BC), obsessed as he was by the desire for kingly magnificence. Habakkuk's words are not specific and it is difficult to be certain, but, as we saw last week, Jeremiah was scathing in his criticism of this king's ostentatious luxury: 'Though your cedar is so splendid, does that prove you a king?' (Jeremiah 22:15, REB). Israel's ideal of kingship was exemplified by Jehoiakim's predecessor, Josiah: 'He judged the cause of the poor and needy; then it was well' (Jeremiah 22:16).

The Babylonians' brutal treatment of conquered nations arose from their desire to display sheer, unadulterated power, but their glory, transient like all human power, would end in shame. The image the prophet uses to depict the humiliation of this arrogant nation is that of unprotected nakedness. In contrast to the Greeks, the Israelites were embarrassed by nakedness and regarded it as shameful. Only in the pristine innocence of the garden of Eden, before the act of disobedience, 'the man and his wife were both naked, and were not ashamed' (Genesis 2:25).

Yet still Habakkuk hasn't finished with contemptuous words against arrogance and self-regarding complacency. He draws on the image of a drunken orgy, a familiar metaphor in the Old Testament, to portray the desperation and chaos of the doomed, whether society or an individual—

a picture made more terrifying by its association with the 'cup of God's wrath' (see Psalm 75:8).

Habakkuk's words end on a note of doom. Thank God, though, that the Old Testament speaks not only of God's cup of wrath but also of the 'cup of salvation', symbolised for Christians by the cup that Jesus shared at the last supper. One psalmist, overwhelmed with thanksgiving, asks, 'What shall I return to the Lord for all his bounty to me? I will lift up the cup of salvation and call on the name of the Lord' (Psalm 116:12–13). Can we do anything less?

2 Lifeless splendour

Habakkuk 2:18–20

Habakkuk has reached the climax of his 'woes'. Here is a brief picture of idol-worship with powerful wordplay (lost in translation), shattering in its ultimate contrast with the true God (v. 20). So much violence and bloodshed, so much brutality and unbridled lust—and so much folly! What a limited vision it is that sees no farther than its own handiwork, satisfied to rest its confidence in the product of its own skilful craft, its own ability! Impressive it may be, this gorgeous object of gold and silver, but it lacks the one thing necessary for life and action—breath. From the beginning of Genesis, with its story of the making of Adam from the clay of the ground, through Ezekiel's vision of dry bones clothed with skin, flesh and sinews, to Paul's sermon in Athens ('[God] the universal giver of life and breath—indeed of everything', Acts 17:25, REB), the Bible affirms that there is no life without the breath of God. With striking alliteration, the prophet describes the splendid idol not as a god (*elohim*) but as a mute idol (*elilim illemim*).

But the Lord... (v. 20). There is another actor in the drama, a new factor in the situation. Habakkuk has no need to spell out the difference between the lifeless artefact and the living Lord. The contrast is complete. The Lord is not embodied in images, however costly, but is worshipped in his holy temple with its dark, empty sanctuary, the Holy of Holies. This God is holy and awe-inspiring, the universal God. It is not the Lord who is silent but the worshippers, hushed in solemnity in his presence (the

Hebrew word *has* echoes the sound of hushing). He is wholly other, distinct from his creation—and here he is in his temple, with the implication that he has come as judge of all the earth.

The audience of this passage is not identified. The subject matter concerns both Babylonians and native Israelites, for they too succumbed to the temptation to seek a God whom they could see, whose nearness they could feel. But the Old Testament is adamant: God the Creator cannot be represented by anything that he has made, except only by humankind, male and female, made in his image, even though that image has been marred and all too often hidden and forgotten.

Here is Habakkuk's challenge today. What are our idols? Materialism, perhaps—ambitions, even relationships usurping God's place. Where is the renewing, revitalising power to be found?

'Breathe on me, breath of God, fill me with life anew' (Edwin Hatch).

3 Past mercies, present faith

Habakkuk 3:1–2

Habakkuk began with prayer and ends with prayer. But what a world of difference between the two! The first was a complaint to a silent God; the second is a proclamation of God's greatness, a God who takes action. Trusting in this unchangeable God, Habakkuk commits himself in utter confidence for the future.

These two verses are a model of brevity in prayer. Habakkuk knows of the past by hearsay, second-hand, but his faith is immediate, first-hand and deeply personal, and his prayer is urgent. It is prayer for the present moment, offered on the community's behalf. Here is the prophet's role as intercessor for his people, having first faithfully brought the searing light of God's word to bear on their disregard of his commandments.

Right at the start of his prayer, the prophet makes an implicit confession of faith. God is not the God of past memories only, a God of history and of hearsay. He is the living Lord of the present moment, of Habakkuk's and his people's own present. This is no deity to be manipulated, guaranteed to be at the disposal of his people, come what may. He is an awesome God, yet approachable in the boldness of faith. God is not to be trifled with. Habakkuk knows of his 'wrath' (v. 2)—not the emotion of petty anger but the revulsion of God's holiness against all injustice and oppression. He knows, too, of God's mercy, for judgment is never God's last word but is always the pathway to transformation and salvation.

Habakkuk's prayer, so psalm-like in its form, suggests that the book was associated originally with liturgical worship. Like the psalms and our Christian hymns and songs, the prayer is non-specific, appropriate for many situations. 'Shigionoth' in the title is of uncertain meaning, probably indicating the appropriate tune or mood of the music. Psalms were a regular component of Israel's worship, sung by an individual or choir with musical accompaniment, keeping alive (then as now) the memory of God's saving acts. But hearsay is not enough. Spiritual life thrives on present experience: 'I have heard…I stand in awe, O Lord, of your work', says Habakkuk, and then he pleads, 'In our own time revive it; in our own time make it known' (v. 2).

What more appropriate prayer for us as we meet each new day with eyes open to see God's presence with us?

4 The glory of the invisible God

Habakkuk 3:3–7

Habakkuk's poetry throbs with his awesome vision of God's glory. This is no God in human image—superman writ large, a deity to be manipulated or wooed by human devotion—but one whose glory fills all things, all space, both heaven and earth. God is invisible and indescribable. No image can represent him. The nearest the prophet-poet can come to describing divine glory is by likening it to the brilliant blazing sun, and perhaps the dazzling lightning ('rays came forth from his hand', v. 4). God's power is controlled, hidden in his hand until he chooses to unleash it.

It is interesting that God is described as coming not from Jerusalem but, drawing on Israel's more ancient traditions, from the southern desert. Teman and Mount Paran (v. 3) were areas through which Israel travelled on its desert journey from Egypt to the promised land. The Lord is a God of movement—not static, not tied to a particular location, but journeying with his people. The link with the south may also represent

Israel's practical experience: the sirocco, blowing from the southern desert, heralded the season's welcome change and the approach of the life-giving autumn rains.

The allusion to pestilence and plague (v. 5) is unclear. These were two Canaanite gods, Deber (pestilence) and Resheph (plague), whose defeat by the god Baal was celebrated in Canaanite poetry. Habakkuk perhaps visualises them as attendant on Yahweh and under his control, just as the fierce sun of the Middle East is both life-giving and destructive. Another view regards them as malevolent deities scattering at God's approach. The mountains shake before the approach of this mighty God. The black bedouin tents of the southern desert shudder as in the fierce winds. Both nature and humans are disturbed by his coming. Yet God himself is unseen; these are only glimpses of his glory.

The Gospels, too, speak of God's glory. In the Synoptics (Matthew, Mark and Luke), Christ is invested at the transfiguration with an overwhelming external radiance, visible to the disciples. In John's Gospel, 'glory' takes on a subtler meaning, manifested supremely in the cross, not as an external radiance visible to physical sight, but in the self-giving of the world's Saviour in suffering, humiliation and death (John 12:27–28; 13:31–32).

5 God's battle against evil

Habakkuk 3:8–15

At first sight, Habakkuk's poetry here is bewildering and disconcerting as he describes the warrior God (arrows and flashing spear, v. 11), until we realise that he is describing God's creative activity as a battle against the forces of chaos. For poetic representations like Habakkuk's, we have to look not at the familiar creation stories in Genesis 1 and 2, but at the Psalms. A glance at Psalm 89:9–14 will reveal the ideas on which Habakkuk is drawing. There God is depicted as defeating the chaos monster, Rahab ('the arrogant one'), and scattering his enemies with his mighty arm. It is clear from the context that the psalmist is thinking of creation, and, in using the words 'rule' and 'throne', he is acclaiming God as King-Creator, keeping in check the forces of chaos.

The ancient Israelites, unlike the Philistines, were not a seagoing people. For Israel, the sea and its raging waters were a terrifying force, symbolic of the primeval waters that God subdued in creation, causing dry land to appear. The language of storm, flashing lightning and crashing waves is drawn from the fierce flashfloods experienced even in the desert. The prophet nowhere confuses God with the forces of nature. As Creator, the Lord is wholly other than his creation. Yet, to speak meaningfully of the power of God whom they could not see, Israel's poets drew by analogy on the mightiest forces they could see—magnificent storms.

In verse 12 Habakkuk turns from nature to history, from natural forces to human chaos. Yet through it all, the purpose of God's coming is clear: he comes with salvation to deliver his people and their anointed king, forerunner of the Messiah and agent of God's rule on earth. The military language is not attractive to us today, but brutal warfare was, and is, a reality. In Habakkuk's time, Judah was faced with a life-threatening crisis. The fall of Jerusalem and its temple was imminent. In this crisis, the prophet celebrates the power of God to save. The oppressors who 'open their jaws to devour their wretched victims' (v. 14, REB) must be defeated if the helpless are to be rescued. Here is the prophet's confident answer to his earlier complaint: God is coming to save his people.

Habakkuk, like other prophets, was a realist. Facing the world's present brutality, he committed the future to the God of justice. We, too, can share his faith as we rejoice in the death-defying, life-transforming power of the cross.

6 From fear to faith

Habakkuk 3:16–19

There is a welter of extreme emotions in these last verses. Habakkuk's vision has a profound effect on him physically. At first he succumbs to weakness and fear as he awaits the calamity that will fall on his enemies. God's advent in judgment is an overwhelming experience to the oppressed as well as the oppressors, even though, for Habakkuk's people, it is the harbinger of salvation. God is awesome in both judgment and redemption.

Then fear changes to faith. Is this because of his quiet, patient waiting for God's intervention (v. 16)? The prophet breaks into a supreme expression of confidence. The people's hopes at the great autumn festival (the Feast of Tabernacles/Booths) focused on their need for the early and latter rains to secure the life-giving harvest. But Habakkuk feels so strongly the overwhelming joy of God's presence that he affirms that even if all shall fail, even if there shall be no harvest, 'Yet I will rejoice in the Lord; I will exult in the God of my salvation' (v. 18).

Habakkuk has learnt that trust in God is not dependent on the signs of his blessing. Ultimately it is God himself, his unseen presence, that is totally satisfying. Habakkuk's is not a grudging, self-humiliating surrender to God. It is joyful, unreserved commitment, for this is the life-giving God who imparts strength and joy, independently of circumstances.

This book, which opened with a querulous complaint against God, ends with the delightful picture of a deer on the mountainside—effortless, liberated and energised. Such is the transformation that can take place, not only after deliverance from troubles and affliction but within them, for God's own presence is the greatest of his gifts. Habakkuk knows that the God whom he worships, the God whom he has dared to confront (1:1–4), is indeed the Lord (v. 19).

Like everyone in ancient Israel, Habakkuk was familiar with the psalms through worship. Scholars have little doubt that Habakkuk's own prayer was intended for liturgical use. His joyful affirmation of faith, independent of circumstance, comes close to the psalmist's total commitment in the words of Psalm 73:25–26: 'Whom have I in heaven but you? And there is nothing on earth that I desire other than you. My flesh and my heart may fail, but God is the strength of my heart and my portion for ever.'

Can we say 'Amen' to this?

Guidelines

We have walked with Habakkuk in his journey from fear to faith. His circumstances have not changed. He still lives in a brutal, precarious world with an uncertain future. What has changed, though, is his consciousness of God's overwhelming presence. Past memories, celebrating in worship God's awesome power as Creator and his triumph over the primeval forces of chaos, ground Habakkuk's present faith and future hope. God is unchanging—the same yesterday, today and for ever—and it is in God himself, not in his gifts and blessings, that Habakkuk's joyful confidence lies.

What past memories of God's gracious intervention in human life can bolster our present faith and future hope?

FURTHER READING

R. Mason, *Zephaniah, Habakkuk, Joel* (Old Testament Guides) (Continuum, 1994).

J.D.W. Watts, *The Books of Joel, Obadiah, Jonah, Nahum, Habakkuk and Zephaniah* (Cambridge Bible Commentaries) (CUP, 1975).

Don't forget to renew your annual subscription to *Guidelines*! If you enjoy the notes, why not also consider giving a gift subscription to a friend or local minister?

SEPT–DEC 2011

Guidelines

Bible study for today's ministry and mission

You will find a subscription order form on pages 155 and 156.
Guidelines is also available from your local Christian bookshop.

Purely and wholly single

The area of love, sex and relationships is one that the church has not always handled terribly well. People outside the church often have all sorts of misunderstandings about what the teaching of the church really is, and some of the controversies of recent years have made it appear as though the church is obsessed with sexual sin.

To hold to the traditional teaching of the church in matters relating to sexual ethics is to live in a radically countercultural way in today's society. The sexual ethics of the world around us have undergone massive changes over the past few decades and have moved very far away from what most Christians would hold as their own values on sexual ethics.

As a single person myself, I am only too well aware that, for single people, it can seem even harder to try to hold on to these traditional teachings, since the choice to be celibate is often ridiculed by those in the world around us. Sadly, some Christian single people also feel that their married Christian friends fail to understand the challenges and issues that they face.

How can single Christian people live sexually pure lives in a world full of sexual temptations? How can single and married people together engage in appropriate, wholesome, loving relationships? How can we be church together—a place of genuine, loving community that welcomes and includes everyone? How can single people stay open to the possibility of finding a marriage partner while at the same time resisting the temptation to put their lives on hold until they find their so-called 'other half'?

These notes focus on singleness and the issues encountered by single people, whether never married, separated, divorced or widowed, but I hope they will still be of relevance to those who are married. All of our churches contain a mixture of single and married people (or at least they should!) so the issues discussed here are relevant to us all.

Over these next two weeks we will look at what the Bible has to say on these issues, and we will consider some of the joys, struggles, blessings and challenges that life as a single Christian in today's society can bring.

Quotations are taken from Today's New International Version of the Bible.

1 Life to the full

John 10:1–10

Jesus, the good shepherd, knows his sheep by name, and his sheep know him. He protects the sheep from those who would seek to harm them. He keeps them safe and he leads them into the good things that he has prepared for them. He is the gate through which they must pass—and, in contrast to the thief, who plans to harm the sheep, Jesus has 'come that they may have life, and have it to the full' (v. 10).

Life to the full—that's the life that we are offered in Jesus Christ. Full life. Complete life. Whole life. Not a life that will be complete only when we find the missing 'other half' of ourselves. Not a life that will be complete once we have got the perfect job, made the perfect home, married the perfect partner and had the perfect children. This is a life that is full and complete and whole simply because it is life in him. Our identity is found in Jesus. God has created each one of us in his own image, to reflect his glory.

A full life is one in which we don't miss out on any of what God has in store for us; where we make the most of every opportunity that he brings our way; where we spend as much time with him as we possibly can; where we seek to share his good news with as many people as we possibly can; where we are comfortable with who he has made us to be; where we are full of joy because of the amazing things he has done for us; where we dedicate each day to him and ask him to use us in it to further his glory.

There can be a risk for many of us, for a variety of reasons, that we miss out on the full life that is on offer. If we are single, we can be tempted to put our lives on hold until we get married. But if we live our lives in that way, we will miss out on so much of what God wants for us.

2 With all your heart

Deuteronomy 6:1–9

Love. As commands go, it's not a bad one, is it? That's what we are commanded to do—and not just to love a little, but to love a lot. We're told to love, in fact, with all that we are, with our heart, soul and strength (v. 5). This command is delivered to God's people and they are exhorted to remember and keep it at all times, and to do everything necessary to ensure that they and their children continue to carry it out. Jesus reiterates to his disciples the central importance of this commandment (Mark 12:30 and Luke 10:27).

To love God with all of our heart speaks to me of the passion that we feel for our God as we receive the immeasurable, unimaginable, incomprehensible passion that he has for us. It speaks of the stirring within all human people to connect with God, and the way that stirring can be satisfied only through giving our lives fully over to him.

To love God with all of our soul speaks to me of the mystery of our relationship with God—the indefinable otherness that is about communion with the creator and sustainer of the universe. It speaks of finding intimacy with God in silent prayer, in the Eucharist, and in reading his word.

To love God with all of our strength speaks to me of a purpose of will, a conscious decision to continue to love and worship God, even when times are hard and we don't feel like it. It speaks, too, of the physical acts of love that we do for God—praising and worshipping him, praying and reading the Bible—as well as those we do for others, such as serving and helping in practical ways, embracing and comforting.

For each of these parts of the command, there is an element of the unconscious. Loving God will sometimes feel like something that simply 'is', as much a part of us as breathing. But there is also an element of the conscious decision. Sometimes, too, it will feel like something that requires an effort of will to achieve.

3 The beloved of the Lord

Deuteronomy 33:12

Have you ever come across part of the Bible that you are convinced you have never set eyes on before but which speaks completely into your life at that moment? That was my experience with today's verse. I was sharing with some friends one day about some struggles I was going through, and especially about the feelings of loneliness in my ministry, and of being overwhelmed by all that there was to do. One of my friends read out this verse, and I was absolutely certain that I had never seen it before, despite the fact that I have read the whole Bible from cover to cover on more than one occasion. This wonderful 'new' discovery spoke powerfully to me at that time.

The context is Moses blessing each of the tribes of Israel before his death. Moving through each of the tribes in turn, he spoke words of blessing from God over them, and these words are the blessing that he spoke to the tribe of Benjamin.

This blessing is a beautiful image of the protective, nurturing love of God. It reminds me of Jesus speaking of his longing to gather the children of Jerusalem into his arms as a hen gathers her chicks under her wings (Matthew 23:37; Luke 13:34). It also makes me think of Jesus telling the parable of the lost sheep, in which the joyful shepherd, having searched for and found his wayward sheep, places it on his shoulders and carries it home to celebrate.

These are very physical, tangible descriptions of love. When someone physically touches us in an appropriate and affirming way, it can help us to feel loved. People who are single or live alone often say that they miss that regular, positive touch. We don't tend to think about being physically 'touched' by God. He is no longer physically present on our planet and so it is not an experience we expect to have in this life. But I think that these words give us an insight into the very physical love that God has for us—a love that shields us and carries us, nurtures us and protects us.

4 Future promise

Luke 18:18–30

The rich young ruler missed out on so much. He came so close, and yet he missed out. His story is a tragic one, because everything that Jesus promised could have been his. He loved God, he kept the commandments, but still he missed out. He simply wasn't able to give up the material things of his life. They were his idols, and, in the final analysis, worshipping them meant more to him than worshipping God.

I often wonder what became of that young man later in life. I like to hope that he realised the error of his ways, and that one day he did, in fact, sell all that he had, give to the poor, and offer his life wholly and unreservedly to Jesus. That would have been a happy ending to the story. But perhaps he did not. Perhaps he continued to allow his life to be ruled by material things until the day he died, unable to accept Jesus' promise that the blessings he would receive upon giving up those things were far greater than any blessing he would receive from holding on to them.

Jesus made a promise to the young man, and he promises the same to us today. He promises that whatever we leave behind in this life in order to follow him, we will be given much more, both in this life and in the life to come. It's not a literal exchange, of course, like a business transaction—as if we give £500 to God's work and next week we receive £1000 back—but it is a real promise. When we give up things in the service of God, he sees our sacrifice, he appreciates it, he values it, and he blesses it.

For those of us who are single and childless, these words can provide comfort. Sometimes it can feel as if we have 'given up' these things because of our decision to live God's way and not to compromise. Yet the promise is clear that we will receive blessings many times more than we would have had if we had chosen a different path from God's best for us.

5 Guard your heart

Proverbs 4:18–27

What becomes of the broken-hearted? Well, the answer surely is that they are hurt and damaged, and, if left untended, the damage can be permanent. But I'm not just talking about the sort of broken heart you might imagine—the broken heart of a jilted lover or of someone experiencing unrequited love.

The word 'heart' appears over 700 times in the Bible. To offer just a few examples, God 'knows the secrets of the heart' (Psalm 44:21); the psalmist asks God to create in him 'a pure heart' (51:10); we are re-assured that God does not judge us by outward appearances but by what is in our hearts (1 Samuel 16:7); and, as we have already seen this week, both Moses and Jesus declare that we are to love God with our heart, soul, mind and strength (Deuteronomy 6:5; Luke 10:27).

So, far from just referring to romantic love, as we tend to think of it today, the biblical word 'heart' has a much wider application. It can refer to the will or intent of a person, a group or even a nation, and it can imply the revelation of someone's true nature. The biblical heart is about emotion, desire, will, intent, intellect and more.

Our hearts can be damaged and broken by the things that happen to us throughout our lives. We can also harden our hearts by the choices we make and the ways in which we live—or we can open our hearts to the healing love of God.

So what does today's passage mean when it tells us to guard our heart (v. 23)? 'Guarding' makes me think of shielding or enclosing our hearts, of protecting them, of taking great care about what goes in and what comes out. What goes into our hearts can be words that other people say to us, whether affirming or damaging; experiences that happen to us and how we deal with them; our sense of our own worth and dignity. What comes out of our hearts can be words that we speak to others, whether in kindness or unkindness; the ways in which we act towards others; our relationships.

An unguarded heart will let in and out things that can cause permanent damage to us and to the people around us. But a guarded heart will take care of what comes and goes, so that neither we nor those we interact with will be harmed, but rather will be blessed and encouraged.

6 Marriage and singleness

1 Corinthians 7:1–11

As I read these words from Paul's letter, I imagine him being a little frustrated, tutting under his breath at the hopelessness of the people he was having to write to, to put them straight on these matters. He does it very nicely, of course, but it's as if he's saying, 'Now come on, just look here. This is how it is—now do it!'

Paul does his best to make his advice as clear and straightforward as he can, but in the midst of it all he uses a little phrase that I think has been much misunderstood over the years. It's this business about our 'gift' that I mean (v. 7). You see, Paul didn't say, 'If you have the gift of singleness, you won't have any sexual desires and you'll be perfectly happy never to get married.' Traditionally, though, his words have been interpreted in that way: if you're not happy being single, then you don't have the gift of singleness, regardless of whether or not you are actually single. But there's a danger here that we come to view the supposed 'gift' of singleness as something we wish we'd kept the receipt for, so that we can return it and exchange it for a different gift.

It is unhelpful to state that if someone doesn't have the gift of singleness, they should get married. Their response is likely to be, 'I would if I could!' It's just not as easy as that. If we are currently single, then we have the 'gift' of singleness from God—it is simply our current state of being. We will retain that gift unless we get married, in which case we will exchange it for the 'gift' of marriage. Both are good; each is different. How liberating it is to read and understand Paul's words in that way! We are free to try to live a full and whole life as a single person, desiring and pursuing marriage if we wish, but not seeing it as a step up from where we currently are.

When we live like that, we will be well on our way to being, as Paul puts it in Philippians 4:11, 'content whatever the circumstances'.

Guidelines

Here are some questions to ponder as you reflect on the Bible passages we have read this week.

- Are you living 'life to the full' (John 10:10) as it is offered in Jesus? If not, what might you do to move towards life in that fullness?
- Do you know yourself to be 'beloved' of God (Deuteronomy 33:12)? If not, you might like to spend some time reflecting on those words and allowing God to speak to you about his love for you.
- Has your heart been damaged or broken because it has been unguarded? Ask God to begin to repair your heart, and to show you how to guard it in the future.
- Can you say, as Paul did, that you are content in all circumstances? If not, why not? Offer your current life situation to God—not the situation you were once in, or would like to be in, but simply where you currently are. Ask him to bring you contentment in that place.

1 It is not good to be alone

Genesis 2:15–25

The opening words of the Bible, describing the creation of the world, are well known to all Christians. We know that Genesis begins with the famous words, 'In the beginning...' We know the poetic rhythm of each different section, starting with 'And God said...' and ending with the numbering of each day. And we know that when God looked at each thing that he had made, he 'saw that it was good'.

Yet, if we read carefully, we will find something that God says is 'not good'—the first time these words are uttered by God. What is it that is 'not good' in God's perfect creation? 'It is not good for the man to be alone' (v. 18).

Notice that God doesn't say, 'It is not good for the man to be single. I will make a wife suitable for him.' What is not good is loneliness, aloneness, and that is what God remedies by creating Eve. So, as human beings, we are made to live in community, in relationship.

Loneliness can very often be an issue for single people. I know it's possible to feel lonely even when you're with other people, and of course some married people sometimes feel lonely. Nevertheless, it is a particular difficulty for single people, especially those who live on their own.

So what can we do about the fact that the Bible warns us that being alone is 'not good'? Clearly, not everyone gets married, and, of those who do, many become single again later in life. Not everyone will want or have the opportunity to live communally with other people. But every one of us has the opportunity to invest in significant relationships, and every one of us has the opportunity to be part of some sort of community.

We see, throughout the Bible, cases of significant non-marital relationships—for example, David and Jonathan, Naomi and Ruth, and Paul and Timothy. We see, too, the importance of community, not least when the church was brought to birth and developed into a group of people who 'were together and had everything in common' (Acts 2:44).

Do you live alone? Would you say that loneliness is an issue for you? If not, do you know of others for whom that might be the case? How might you begin to build or join a community, or encourage others to do so?

2 Church as community

Psalm 68:1–10

God cares for those whom society forgets and fails to care for. God cares for the unloved, the excluded, the outcast. This psalm reminds us that God cares for the fatherless and the widow—those who have lost the human family whose role was to love and care for them. God is able to fulfil that role and provide for all of our requirements for love and affection.

God does even more, though, than simply showing us love himself. He also 'sets the lonely in families' (v. 6): he enables human beings to form communities in which they can love and care for one another, embracing within themselves everyone who is in need of such love.

Some people are married, some have children, some are single, some live with others and some live alone. For all of those people, but perhaps especially for those who are single and live alone, the church should be the place where they experience community. At their best, our churches should work like families, where we all rub along together—old and young, married and single—and all love, support, cherish and care for one another.

Our church should be the one place where we can be sure of finding love, acceptance and support. It should be the place where we can take our pain and struggles and find people to love us through them and pray for us in them. Our fellow Christians, our brothers and sisters in Christ, are surely the very people we ought to be able to rely on to love us unconditionally. We deserve to be loved for who we are, not for who we might be if only we were paired off.

This is an area in which the church should really be miles ahead of the world around us. In our society, the obsession with sex means that people miss out on community, on genuine relationships, where 'family' means more than just the people we're related to. In church, we should know better than this. We should know how to be family for one another.

3 The blessing of solitude

Luke 5:12–16

As we have already seen this week, loneliness can be a particular issue for single people who live on their own. It can be a difficult, painful and uncomfortable experience—but is it possible to turn the pain of loneliness into a blessing? Loneliness is a word we perceive negatively. It speaks of being alone against our will, of struggling with being alone, of wishing we were not alone. Solitude, on the other hand, is a much more positive word. It speaks of being alone through choice, being alone for a purpose. Solitude is something we may choose, in order to reflect—taking time out from the busyness of life to be still. Even if solitude isn't actively chosen, we may be able to decide to turn our aloneness into solitude rather than loneliness.

We see, as we read the Gospels, that there were numerous occasions when Jesus chose to withdraw from the crowds to be by himself. He did this partly in order to be refreshed, to 'recharge his batteries' and gather strength for his next task, but he did it primarily, of course, to spend time with his Father in prayer, to talk to God and listen to God, and simply to be with God.

When we read that Jesus made a habit of doing something regularly, we need to investigate further. We find that these times of withdrawal come either immediately after Jesus has been ministering and giving out to others, or immediately before he is due to teach or heal. He also spent a whole night by himself with God before making the important decision about whom to choose as his closest disciples (Luke 6:12–13). It is plain that, for Jesus, these times of quiet with his Father were vital.

I believe that, as Christians, we all need to follow Jesus' example and seek out times when we and our Father can be together, away from the bustle of our everyday lives. However, I think we need to recognise that single people who live alone have a greater opportunity to make the most of such times and to seek out a deeper level of intimacy with God.

We have a choice. We can allow ourselves to descend into feelings of despair over our loneliness, or we can decide to turn our time alone into the more positive experience of solitude—time spent alone with Jesus. We can see him as our best friend, our brother and our lover. It is our choice as to whether or not we make the most of that opportunity. It's not easy, but it's a decision we can make.

4 Sexual purity

Romans 13:8–14

The world in which we live today can appear to be obsessed with sex. There are so many images and messages relating to sex, and they confront us wherever we turn. Adverts on television and on billboards use sex to sell any and every product, from cars to chocolate to shampoo.

Does it shock us to be exposed to these images every way we turn, or does it feel normal to us because it's what we experience all the time? As a nation, we seem happy not just for ourselves but also for our children to be presented with such images—to be told, implicitly and explicitly, that sex sells, that it's a commodity and a right.

As far as the outside world is concerned, the church appears to veer between two extremes in its attitude towards sex. On one hand, the church is seen as being prudish and old-fashioned in its attitudes, stuck in the outdated view that sex is not to be openly discussed. On the other hand, however, the church is seen as being obsessed with sexual sin, talking about it all the time and viewing it as more serious than any other sort of sin.

The Bible is far from silent on the issue of sex and relationships. The

Bible says very clearly that sex is a good thing, that it is a gift from God, and that it's for enjoyment and the procreation of children. But the Bible also says very clearly that sex is a gift that is given for married people only. The only place for sexual activity is within a committed marriage relationship between a man and a woman.

Paul makes it clear in his letter to the Romans that our sexual behaviour matters. He reminds us of the importance and sanctity of love—that 'love does no harm to its neighbour. Therefore love is the fulfilment of the law' (v. 10). We are warned against sexual immorality and debauchery, because these kinds of behaviour are contrary to the pure life that we are called to live in Christ, and they damage us and the people around us.

Living this way in the 21st-century Western world is to live a profoundly countercultural life, and one that is radically liberating.

5 Whatever is pure

Philippians 4:4–13

Sexual temptation comes from many sources and in many guises. It might be on television, on the internet or in a magazine. To be tempted, in itself, is not a sin. Jesus himself was tempted in every area of life, and yet he was without sin (Hebrews 4:15). That must also be our aim.

What we must do with our sexual temptation, as with every other struggle against sin that we face, is to bring it prayerfully to God. Paul urges us 'in every situation' (v. 6) to pray and seek God. Often we imagine that our sexual temptations are too awful, too shameful to mention out loud to anyone, even to God—but do we imagine that he is not already aware of them? Being tempted to sexual sin is no better or worse than being tempted to any other sort of sin. Sin is just sin—awful, mucky, unpleasant stuff that leads us away from God instead of towards him.

There's nothing clever that can be said about temptation. We are all tempted, and to resist it is really hard. However hard it is, though, the only approach to take is the straightforward one. So, if there's anything we find ourselves doing that we think we wouldn't do if Jesus was standing right there next to us in the flesh, we simply need to stop doing it, right away.

We also need to make sure that if we have made a decision not to fill our minds with something unhelpful, we fill it instead with something helpful. You know what it's like if somebody tells you not to think about elephants? What can you then not get out of your head…? Instead, we need to make a choice to fill our minds with thoughts that are edifying and holy.

What better passage of scripture to meditate on at such times than today's reading? Whenever we are tempted to fill our minds with ideas that are unwholesome and unhelpful, let's remember Paul's command to think about 'whatever is true, whatever is noble, whatever is right, whatever is pure, whatever is lovely, whatever is admirable… excellent or praiseworthy' (v. 8).

If we think it is too hard to turn our backs on all of the temptations of the world around us, we can remind ourselves that 'I can do all this through him who gives me strength' (v. 13).

6 Even Jesus was tempted

Hebrews 4:14–16

Jesus is our great high priest, and, as the writer to the Hebrews tells us, he is not a priest who sits far off from us, looking down in judgment. Rather, he is a priest who has been where we are and done the things that we do, and, because of this, he is able fully to understand all of our human experiences.

We often talk about the incarnation when we want to remind ourselves that Jesus experienced pain as he hung on the cross and so can empathise with us in our pain. We remember that Jesus wept over the death of his friend Lazarus, and so he can weep with us in our grief of bereavement. We remember that Jesus was rejected by his friends and neighbours when he spoke in the synagogue (Mark 6:3), and so he understands when our friends and family reject and ridicule us for speaking out for him.

We even mention that Jesus was tempted to sin, and, when we do that, the passage we most often cite is the one we entitle 'The Temptation of Jesus' (Matthew 4:1–11; Mark 1:12–13; Luke 4:1–13). But how often, I wonder, do we really consider the consequences of the assertion in

Hebrews that Jesus was 'tempted in every way, just as we are'?

I want to suggest that if that statement is to have any truth at all, then it must mean that Jesus was tempted to sexual sin, because we human beings are certainly tempted in that way. We know, of course, that the sentence ends, '… yet he did not sin', but that does not negate the first part of the sentence.

I find it enormously helpful to know that Jesus was tempted to sexual sin, and yet I also find it profoundly challenging. It is helpful because it reminds me that in this area, as in every other area of my life, Jesus has been there and he truly understands. It is challenging for exactly the same reason. I cannot hide behind my temptations and say, 'Ah, but Lord, you just don't know what it's like for me.' He knows, I believe, exactly what it is like. And so we must strive to be without sin in this area of our lives, as in every other, if we are truly seeking to become more like Christ.

Guidelines

Here are some questions to consider, stemming from the Bible passages we have read this week.

- Does your church function as a true 'community'? If not, what might you do to foster a sense of community within it?
- Is loneliness an issue for you? Do you need to be proactive in finding communities to be part of? Do you need to bring your loneliness to God and ask him to lead you to a person or persons with whom you can build relationship?
- Do you see time spent alone as a burden of loneliness or a blessing of solitude? Ask God to show you ways in which you could begin to see time spent alone with him as a way to experience deeper levels of intimacy with him.
- Is sexual temptation an issue for you? Are there areas in which you need to change your patterns of behaviour? Do you need to find a trusted friend to confide in and be accountable to?

FURTHER READING

Al Hsu, *The Single Issue* (IVP, 1997).

Philip B. Wilson, *Being Single: Insights for Tomorrow's Church* (DLT, 2005).

Daniel

The book of Daniel is rather like the book of Revelation. In both there are parts that are well known and liked (the letters to the churches and the vision of the new Jerusalem in Revelation; the fiery furnace and the lions' den in Daniel) but there are also large parts that are deliberately overlooked. I guess that few of us have, for example, heard many sermons on the vision of the ram and the goat in Daniel 8.

The text itself is unique within the Old Testament because half of it is written in Aramaic (the language of the Jews at the time of Daniel and afterwards), rather than Hebrew. The Aramaic portion begins quite logically in 2:4 as the words of a speech, but nobody has come up with a convincing explanation as to why the Aramaic then continues, long after the speech is finished, through to the end of chapter 7.

Much energy has been spent on the issue of dating Daniel. There is no doubt that it is set during the exile of the Jews in Babylon, between the reigns of the Babylonian King Nebuchadnezzar and the Persian King Cyrus (roughly between 587 and the 530s BC). In particular, the first half of the book contains 'court tales', very clearly set in this period. However, the second half of the book, particularly chapters 8—12, seems to focus on the desecration of the temple by another king, Antiochus Epiphanes, in 168BC. Furthermore, the two halves have very different attitudes towards the non-Jewish rulers. In chapters 1—6 it is very clear that the Jews can flourish under foreign rule; in chapters 7—12, foreign rule is the evil enemy. This leads many to believe that chapters 1—6, with their message that foreign rulers are no threat, could not have originated from the period of Antiochus, and that chapters 8—12 cannot originate from the earlier, far more 'pro-foreign rulers' period.

Bogging ourselves down in arguments over the origins of the text is unlikely to be fruitful, however, and is not necessary. Daniel is scripture. Some of it is hard to understand, and yet, in Paul's words, all scripture was written 'for our instruction' (Romans 15:4). Therefore, we approach Daniel with the expectation that God will speak to us through it today.

These notes have been prepared using the New Revised Standard Version of the Bible.

1 Living in exile

Daniel 1

How do you live in a nation that does not follow your religious beliefs? This is the question at the heart of the book of Daniel, set as it is during the period when the Jews lived in exile in Babylon (2 Chronicles 36:17–23). It is a question of perennial importance because Christians are encouraged to see their life as a form of 'exile' from their true home (Philippians 3:20; 1 Peter 1:1). However, it has come into sharper focus as the culture and legal framework within Britain (and other Western countries) has moved away from its Christian roots. In areas such as the beginning and end of life, and discrimination laws, Christians have begun to feel that there are, or soon will be, conflicts between their Christian beliefs and the law.

Three points emerge from Daniel 1. First, we see that God is still at work, even though the people are in exile (v. 2: 'The Lord let…'; v. 17: the young men gained their wisdom from God, not from their Babylonian education). This might not seem a great revelation to us, but it is almost impossible for us to comprehend the trauma for the Jews—whose religion had been based on a belief in God's gift of the land and on worship in the temple—when the temple was destroyed and they were removed from their land. Despite the complete collapse of their religious framework, God was still at work. By the same token, perhaps we should not worry too greatly about the 'decline of Christendom' or the current decline in many churches.

Second, we might ask: what was the danger faced by Daniel and the others? They were not being persecuted, and they had no problem about serving the Babylonian king and seeking the welfare of the Babylonian state. In so doing, however, they were in danger of being absorbed into its culture and losing all that was distinctive about their own. It is not clear why there was a problem with the food (vv. 8, 12), for the Jewish law does not require vegetarianism. Perhaps they feared that the meat and wine had been offered to Babylonian gods, or perhaps they were simply displaying the fact that they were not dependent on the king's favour, because they served another.

Third, the result was not seen as a triumph over non-Jewish Babylon. The men's loyalty to God worked for their benefit and for the benefit of the society in which they lived (vv. 15–20). The two were not opposed. We might take heart from this: living in accordance with God's will today is also good for our society, even if that society no longer sees itself as based on Christian teaching.

2 God is supreme

Daniel 2

This story of the statue is the dominant story in the whole of Daniel, setting the tone for the rest of the book. A statue reappears in chapter 3, it has similarities to the tree in chapter 4, and it seems to be the starting point for the vision of chapter 7, which itself leads on into chapters 8—12. Indeed, the statue is perhaps best viewed not as representing different aspects of Nebuchadnezzar's kingdom, but as a picture of his dynasty, starting in glory and gradually decaying. Thus it encompasses the whole chronology of the book of Daniel, and acts as a stepping stone to the idea of 'successive kingdoms' that comes to the fore in chapter 7.

Here in chapter 2, as the text moves into Aramaic (see Introduction) it also moves into full 'storytelling mode': the text is full of colour and tension. We might also see the complexity of the origins of the book of Daniel in the tension between the way Daniel is introduced here (as one of the wise men, vv. 12–13, 18, but unknown to the king, v. 25) and the picture at the end of chapter 1 (vv. 18–20).

Two themes emerge from this chapter. First, there is the importance of visions and dreams and the power to interpret them. God is called the 'revealer of mysteries' (vv. 28, 29, 47). This points us back to Joseph, who found himself in exile in Egypt and rose to high office because God revealed to him the meaning of dreams. This link between Egypt and the Babylonian exile is fundamentally a hopeful one, because God rescued his people from Egypt and so will do again from Babylon (see, for example, Isaiah 43:14–17). The interpretation of dreams and visions is crucial in

Daniel. Here it also connects with the rescue of the Jews (2:18), deliverance being the theme of chapters 1, 3 and 6. This is not just a clever trick, for God's ability to 'reveal mysteries' demonstrates that he is in control of the future.

Second, expanding upon the first theme, is the theme of God's sovereignty. Even if things appear to be getting worse and the kingdom is decaying from glorious gold to worthless clay, God's rule will be established. Meanwhile, God's people can remain loyal to him while finding high office in and contributing to the welfare of non-Jewish regimes, for even there God remains sovereign, as we will see in chapters 3—6.

It is good to be reminded that despite appearances and our own inability to understand, God is sovereign, reigns supreme and holds the future in his hands.

3 God can save

Daniel 3

This depiction of Jewish life in exile is similar to that in chapter 6 and in the book of Esther. We should not see the king as being intentionally hostile to the Jews. The statue (a link to chapter 2) and the command to worship it (vv. 4–7) are surely meant to demonstrate political loyalty and unity in a diverse 'world empire'; they are not intended to cut across religious practice. But of course they do cut across Jewish religious practice because of Judaism's insistence that worship must be limited to the one supreme Creator God. Thus we see the complexity of the believer's life in a society that runs on a completely different basis. The state may not intend to pressurise or persecute on religious grounds, but its worldview and fundamental understanding are so different that, as here, a crisis develops.

Within this context, mischief makers emerge (vv. 8–12). The king himself is not hostile (although verses 13 and 19–22 remind us that kings are erratic and best avoided); others cause trouble, twisting the situation for their own benefit. We might compare the situation of Christians in countries such as Pakistan, where there is no official persecution but where Islamic blasphemy laws can be exploited by those with a grudge, to the great harm of Christians.

Whatever the cause of the clash or the king's original intention, the three men find themselves facing a head-on collision between their faith and the state (vv. 15, 28). The message of the story is uncompromising. If the state demands idolatrous worship, the believers must resist. The men's response to the king is double-edged (vv. 17–18), for while they express hope that God will rescue them, they also make clear that even if he does not, they will still stay loyal to him. We see here the emergence of the idea of martyrdom. Such an idea tends to require a belief in an afterlife, where wrongs can be finally put right and the martyr rewarded—which is indeed what we find in Daniel 12:1–4, one of the few clear expressions of this belief in the Old Testament.

However, this story does not end with martyrdom. God's action proves that the God whom the men serve 'is able to deliver us from the furnace of blazing fire and out of your hand, O king' (v. 17), as the king himself later testifies publicly (v. 28). The simplicity of the story is challenging, for we can easily think of cases where God does not seem to rescue in this way. Nevertheless, the point is clear that, although much in chapters 1—6 suggests that there need not be a clash between state power and God's requirements, if the state seeks to usurp God's place, resistance and trust in God are the only possible response. Would we have the courage to make that response?

4 Pride

The format of this chapter is intriguing: it is a first-person testimony from King Nebuchadnezzar himself. It appears fantastical—wishful thinking on the part of a Jewish writer, imagining perhaps how God might have humbled the great Babylonian king who sacked Jerusalem. However, there is an interesting piece of Babylonian history to which it may connect. The last king of Babylon, Nabonidus, did withdraw from society to a desert oasis (called Tayma) for many years, leaving behind his son Belshazzar to rule. This was very unusual and remains unexplained historically. A text found in the Dead Sea Scrolls (4QPrNab) tells, supposedly in Nabonidus' own words, how he was afflicted by God for seven years in Teiman, until he prayed to God, and an exorcist who was one of the Jewish exiles forgave his sin. Perhaps an original account of the encounter of an unknown Jew with a little-known Babylonian king, who did indeed withdraw from Babylonian society for an unexplained reason, was later incorporated into the Daniel story (for more on Nabonidus/Belshazzar, see the notes on Daniel 5).

The point of the story is straightforward. However powerful the Babylonian King Nebuchadnezzar might appear, it is God who is sovereign (v. 3); it is God alone who can take away and restore kingdoms (vv. 31, 36). Arrogance is an offence against God. From a king it is, in effect, a form of blasphemy—an attempt to usurp God's place (v. 30). Perhaps there is a hint in verse 11 ('its top reached to heaven') of the tower of Babel, which was the ultimate expression of man's arrogance, also set in Babylonia (compare Genesis 11:4).

The warning against arrogance is one that all of us can take to heart, for while the king's words ('Is this not magnificent Babylon, which I have built as a royal capital by my mighty power and for my glorious majesty?': v. 30) may seem distant from our experience, in essence they were a claim that all his success was his own doing and for his own sake. In our own lives it is easy to make, essentially, the same claim. It is easy to pay lip service to the idea that God is sovereign but, in practice, work on the basis that our achievements are our own work, with the odd bit of help from God.

It is also notable that the king is forgiven and restored. All he need do, it seems, is recognise God's lordship. The simplicity of this idea, although it is in keeping with the thrust of the gospel (see, for example, the parables in Luke 15, and Luke 23:39–43), may also challenge the church's seemingly inexhaustible ability to make things more complicated.

5 God is judge

Daniel 5

This story follows on from the previous one, for King Belshazzar is said to be the son of Nebuchadnezzar (v. 2). Traditionally, this has caused great difficulty for scholars, who could find no reference to a Babylonian king named Belshazzar; in addition, no son of Nebuchadnezzar, the conqueror of Jerusalem, was king of Babylon at the time when Babylon itself was conquered (v. 30). However, there was a Belshazzar, son of the last king of Babylon (Nabonidus), who ruled in his father's place when the king withdrew from society. This would help to explain verses 10–12, for 'the queen' there is not Belshazzar's wife but his mother, Nabonidus' wife, and thus a figure of authority. While our best understanding of the history of the end of the Babylonian empire is that Nabonidus returned (as in Daniel 4:36), it appears that Belshazzar then ruled alongside him and was actually in command of Babylon when it fell. Thus we can see a context for chapters 4 and 5 of Daniel within the final period of the Babylonian empire, even if there is some confusion between Nebuchadnezzar and Nabonidus and over the details of Belshazzar's position.

The story begins with a reminder of the sacrilege and arrogance of the Babylonian king Nebuchadnezzar in taking the vessels from the Jerusalem temple into his own possession. In the story that follows, it is Belshazzar's sacrilege that is highlighted (v. 23) and results in judgment (vv. 26–28). However, there is a more general sense that judgment is falling on Nebuchadnezzar's dynasty for the sacrilege begun by Nebuchadnezzar and continued by those who followed him. In the imagery of the statue in chapter 2, the whole statue, made up of successive decaying rulers, is an affront to God and is destroyed by him. This also helps us understand the confusion over the rulers of Babylon. Within the book of Daniel, Nebuchadnezzar conquers Jerusalem and, because of his arrogance in exalting himself over God, his son is himself conquered. Historians may suggest that the line of succession between the conqueror and the conquered was more stretched out than that, with other kings in between, but theologically the point is made. Nebuchadnezzar destroyed Jerusalem by God's will, but then his son (his descendant or dynasty) was destroyed by God's will for their joint arrogance.

Most of us feel disconnected from the concept of sacrilege. Perhaps a point of connection for us is to think of the earth. Just as the temple objects in this story were God's property but were misused by Belshazzar as he arrogantly took them for himself, the earth itself is the Lord's (Psalm 24:1) but similarly we often take it as our own and misuse it.

6 The lions' den

Daniel 6

This story about Daniel has many similarities to the story about Shadrach, Meshach and Abednego in chapter 3. In both, there is no true clash between the ruler and the Jews: the problem comes from mischief makers (explicitly here in vv. 4, 22). Once again we are reminded that, in principle, God's people can live and thrive under 'non-believing' rulers, even if times of crisis come.

In comparison with chapter 3, though, the Persian king is more favourably portrayed here. He raises Daniel to high office (v. 2) and does not want him to die (vv. 14, 16, 18). This is in keeping with all Jewish portrayals of Persian rule: while the Babylonians took them into exile, the Persians allowed them to return. Benevolent or not, however, there is still the danger of a clash between the state's laws and God's laws. The idea of the 'law of the Medes and the Persians which cannot be revoked' (v. 8) is very clever, for it creates the drama of the story while also setting up the underlying theological point. Which of the two laws—the law of the Medes and Persians (the greatest world empire at the time) and the law of God—is really unchangeable?

As in chapter 3, this story explores the limits of acceptable obedience to the state. Daniel is a high official who serves the king well; it is assumed throughout that God's people can flourish within secular government and society. Yet, when the state forbids worshipping God, their duty is clear. Indeed, the undramatic tone of verse 10 makes the point particularly strongly. There is no anguish or deliberation on Daniel's part, because there is no decision for him to agonise over.

Chapters 4 and 5, immediately followed by this one, provide two sides of the story. First we see that God will bring down rulers who challenge him, and then we see what is required of God's people in the meantime. They are to serve willingly and flourish under states that do not acknowledge God, while retaining a primary loyalty to God in the unlikely situation of a genuine clash between the state's laws and God's. The resolution of such situations is in God's hands.

The overall effect is to give us confidence in our engagement with society. God will look after his own glory; we do not need to defend him.

We can work enthusiastically for the 'welfare of the city where I have sent you' (Jeremiah 29:7), but we might wish to ponder the limits of such commitment to our society. What counts as a clash with God's laws? Interestingly, in Daniel the only such clashes depicted are the most blatant possible: demanding the worship of non-gods (ch. 3) and forbidding the worship of God (ch. 6).

Guidelines

These first six chapters of Daniel have given a generally positive portrayal of life in a nation that does not follow one's religious beliefs. There need not be a clash between commitment to a state or society and commitment to God. Christians can, and should, be working to prosper the place where they live. However, the stories have also explored the boundaries—the need to retain one's distinctiveness (compare Matthew 5:13–16) and the need to worship God alone. Most of us probably lean towards one side of this balance or the other.

Are you someone who is always likely to 'compromise', to avoid any sense of a clash between our faith and the society in which we live? Do you need to ponder again the example of these heroes who had the courage to stand for God and trust in God's sovereignty?

Alternatively, are you someone who always sees the relationship between our faith and our society through the lens of opposition, assuming conflict? Do you need to ponder again the suggestion in these chapters that there are very few areas in which our faith should conflict with wider society, and that in general we can flourish within it?

1 Suffering and vindication

Daniel 7

This chapter marks a departure from chapters 1—6. The narrative is now told in the first person. Now Daniel does not interpret dreams; he receives them, and other, heavenly, beings need to interpret them for him

(vv. 2, 16). Furthermore, the vision dominates, while in chapters 1—6 the visions are only ever part of a story. 'Court tales' that include interpretation of dreams have given way to apocalyptic literature.

When Daniel's vision is read alongside its two interpretations (vv. 15–18, 19–27), a basic story emerges. There are successive world empires, depicted as 'beasts'. The first three are not necessarily seen in negative terms—particularly the first one, which has a human mind. However, the fourth, with its 'horns', is explicitly said to be different (v. 23). This fourth 'kingdom' is arrogant (vv. 8, 20) and blasphemous (v. 25) and makes war with the holy ones: that is, one presumes, it persecutes God's people. Because we are familiar with the term 'son of man' to describe Jesus, we can easily miss the way that the 'son of man' or 'human being' in verse 13 functions. A comparison of verses 14, 18 and 27 makes clear that this 'human being' is a dream-world representation of God's people, just as the beasts are a dream-world representation of pagan empires.

Thus we see that three world empires will pass, and the fourth will persecute God's people. In the end, though, God will intervene (v. 9) and bring judgment on the arrogant kingdom, while vindicating his people and establishing their rule. In effect, the fall will be reversed: the 'human' will rule over the 'beasts', not the other way around, as was intended by God (Genesis 1:28). Chapters 1—6 have illustrated that, in general, God's people can flourish under pagan empires: it is only the fourth beast, and really only its tenth horn, that persecutes them. But such times of terrible suffering can come, for a period.

The details can be seen as suggesting that the arrogant king is Antiochus Epiphanes, who desecrated the Jewish temple in 168BC. However, this limits the meaning. More fundamentally, the story admits that persecution and suffering will come to God's people, and evil may seem to prevail (vv. 7, 21), but God is still in control (v. 25b: God gives the people into the fourth beast's hands for a defined period of time). In the end he will vindicate his people and establish justice. This story finds its clearest expression in the death and resurrection of Jesus, but finds reapplication throughout history. Perhaps we can identify situations in our own life that follow the same structure: in some cases vindication may already have come; in others we are still suffering but trusting God.

2 The unimaginable happens

Verses 10–13 describe the most unimaginable horror for the pious Jewish reader. The Jerusalem temple is 'trampled' by an arrogant foreign king and the sacrifices are stopped. This would be a terrible sacrilege—all that is precious to them being treated with contempt—but it's more than that. The fact that the king is able to do this suggests that God is either powerless or has abandoned them. Furthermore, without the temple, what are they? The Jews are bound together by their common religion. If that religion is destroyed or found wanting, there will be nothing left. Truly this would have been a sacrilege causing complete desolation (v. 13).

Again, the details (vv. 3–9) point to the arrogant king being Antiochus Epiphanes. The ram is the Persian empire, and the goat the Greek empire, with the 'great horn' being Alexander the Great, whose empire was split, after his death, into four. One of the four parts was ruled by the Seleucid kings, who included Antiochus. All of this raises the question of when chapter 8 was written. Some insist that it was written by Daniel during the exile (500s BC) as predictive prophecy; others assert that it must have been written between 168 and 165BC—after Antiochus took the temple, but before it was retaken by the Jews (hence the detail in the text up to the point when the temple is desecrated, but vagueness thereafter: v. 25).

It's not clear how productive such arguments are, if we are reading the chapter to hear God's word to us now. We might focus instead on the Jews' experience of the unimaginable horror actually happening, something that rips apart their whole way of understanding the world. What would be our equivalent? The most precious things in the world for me are my two boys: if they were to die, my world would come crashing down, and my traumatised mind would grieve over the question of whether God was weak or whether he just didn't care. The approach of this chapter is to describe a world in which terrible evil happens but is somehow contained within God's plan, such that in the end God's rule will be asserted. In this context we can understand the logic behind telling the story of the goat and the ram. The unimaginable horror is not a random catastrophe but fits within an ongoing story known to God, which reaches God's chosen conclusion.

Of course, this does not mean that the horror suddenly becomes manageable. Daniel can't understand it without God's aid (vv. 15–16); it is called the 'period of wrath' (v. 19) and the whole thing makes him sick, dismayed and confused (v. 27). Yet he, and we, are encouraged to believe that, in some way, such horror can be contained within and overcome by God's purposes.

3 How long?

Once again we find Daniel wrestling to try to understand God's plan, but now the stimulus is not a vision but the words of Jeremiah (an extremely rare example of one Old Testament text referring to another).

Daniel is still thinking about the desecration by Antiochus described in his vision. His difficulty, though, is that this does not fit into his scheme of history. His understanding, shaped by Jeremiah (v. 2; see Jeremiah 25:11–12; 29:10), is that the people were sent into exile for their sin for 70 years, after which they would be restored and the temple rebuilt (the 'return' under Zerubbabel, Ezra 1:8–11, did take place roughly 70 years later). But in that case, in the time of Antiochus long after this restoration, they should be living free and content, enjoying God's blessing, not enduring the desecration of the temple.

For Daniel, the only way of understanding the events under Antiochus is that the 'period of wrath' is continuing (v. 16; 8:19); the people's sin, which caused the exile to begin, has not yet been atoned for, and so, even if they have physically returned to the land, they remain in spiritual exile. Thus the overall theological scheme is preserved: the event under Antiochus is part of the same, well-understood, exile because of sin, from which God will rescue them.

What, then, of Jeremiah's '70 years' (v. 2)? Many hundreds of years separate the fall of Jerusalem to Babylon and the desecration of the temple by Antiochus. Why is the exile continuing so long? Why is the restoration, God's action, delayed?

The answer is a reworking of the concept of Jeremiah's 70 years, in which they are transformed into 70 weeks of years (70 x 7), or ten weeks of weeks of years (vv. 24–27). Thus there is a first period of a week of weeks of years (49 years) of the exile itself, then eight more weeks of weeks of years (392 years) of Jerusalem being rebuilt in troubled times. Then, at the beginning of the tenth and final week of weeks, the events involving Antiochus happen. The sacrifices will stop for half a week—that is, three and a half years (the 'time, two times and half a time' of Daniel 7:25)—'until the decreed end is poured out upon the desolator' (v. 27). The restoration may seem delayed, but in fact all is happening by clock-work, to a fixed plan.

Such an attempt to schematise history according to a pattern of numbers does little for most people today, but we can understand the theological point: it is an attempt to make sense of God's apparent delay in establishing justice. Do we share the anguish of seeing pain and suffering in our world? How do we make sense of it?

4 It is a fight

Daniel 10

Once again we begin with Daniel trying to understand what has happened. We are not told what Daniel is 'mourning' (v. 2). In his historical context, we might assume it to be the fact that he is in exile and the temple destroyed, but it may be reapplied easily to other situations or events. The descriptions of Daniel's physical and emotional state (vv. 3, 8–10, 15–18) are particularly vivid and suggest that visionary experience underlies the account.

The vision and the interpretation that follows offer a different approach to understanding world events and the apparent lack of answer from God. There is a battle going on between spiritual forces or beings (vv. 13, 20–21). In this chapter the battle seems to be focused particularly on opposition to Daniel's receiving revelation (vv. 12–14), so the spiritual beings could still be seen as 'messengers from God'. However, the talk of 'princes' and the reappearance of Michael in 12:1 as 'the protector of your people' point towards a wider concept of spiritual beings who in some sense represent, or work on behalf of, or even control, the destiny of people or nations. While this is a new concept within the Old Testament, we can see connections with the 'commander of the army of the Lord' in Joshua 5:14 and, less closely, with 2 Kings 6:17.

The same idea is picked up in the New Testament—for example, in Ephesians 6:12 ('For our struggle is not against enemies of blood and flesh, but against the rulers, against the authorities, against the cosmic powers of this present darkness, against the spiritual forces of evil in the heavenly places') and 2 Corinthians 4:4 ('the god of this world has blinded the minds of the unbelievers, to keep them from seeing the light of the gospel').

Many of us worry about such language of 'spiritual warfare', conscious of its use within various forms of extremism and concerned about suggestions of militarism. We might also be aware of the ease with which it can descend into a form of dualism, with two 'gods' opposing each other, one good and one bad— which contradicts the biblical declaration of God's sovereignty. However, whether we are comfortable with it or not, it is certainly included in the biblical picture as part of an explanation of suffering: things are not as God wants; he is working (fighting) to restore the world; he will win, but victory is not immediate or easy. This can connect with our own experience of working for justice, where fatalism (the idea that 'God will do it') is not sufficient. We need to work alongside God, to join with him in the battle against evil.

5 Loyalty

Daniel 11

Once again we read a history of the empires that fought over and around Israel in the period between the exile and Antiochus' rule. Here the focus is on the activities of the Seleucid dynasty in Syria (the 'king of the north') and its wars particularly with the Ptolemy dynasty in Egypt (the 'king of the south'), in which, at one point, the newly emerging power of Rome involved itself (the 'kittim', v. 30). Again the story is told leading up to Antiochus' desecration of the temple (v. 31).

This time, however, there is a new element, which is the repeated reference to some Jews who support Antiochus: 'those who forsake the holy covenant' (v. 30); 'he shall seduce with intrigue those who violate the covenant; but the people who are loyal to their God shall stand firm and take action' (v. 32); 'many shall join them insincerely' (v. 34).

This picture seems to be confirmed by 1 Maccabees, a text in the Old Testament Apocrypha, which deals with the crisis caused by Antiochus. It says, 'In those days certain renegades came out from Israel and misled many saying, "Let us go and make a covenant with the Gentiles around us" … so they built a gymnasium in Jerusalem according to Gentile custom, and removed the marks of circumcision, and abandoned the holy covenant. They joined with the Gentiles and sold themselves to do evil' (1 Maccabees 1:11–15).

It is probably fair to assume that those involved did not think they were 'abandoning the covenant' but rather that they had a 'less separationist' view of Judaism and were more content to assimilate. The earlier part of Daniel 11 illustrates well why this would have been attractive or seemed sensible. Israel was at the mercy of forces far larger than itself, caught on the frontier between the 'king of the north' and the 'king of the south'. Israel had an insignificant role in this globalised world: did it really make sense for it to become a ghetto? Nevertheless, the view from within Daniel is clear that the Israelites were mistaken to do this, and were acting against God.

Thus a new aspect is added to the issues of suffering and endurance. When coping with a life or a situation in which God seems absent, not only do we cry out 'How long?' and recognise that we are involved in a fight, but we also have to resist the temptation to become gradually worn down, to lose our distinctiveness and live as if we didn't know and trust God. Job was encouraged to 'curse God, and die' (Job 2:9)—to stop maintaining his belief in God's goodness in the face of seemingly contrary evidence—but he resisted. Daniel 11 encourages us, too, to resist such temptation and remain loyal to God.

6 Justice will come

Daniel 12

Once again we are wrestling with the events of Antiochus' desecration of the temple. Even if the first verse seems less precise and, perhaps, of wider application ('a time of anguish'), verses 7 and 11 focus on the desecration. The two different numbers of days in verses 11 and 12 are intriguing (8:14 gives a different number again), though all are in the region of three and a half years (7:25; 9:27; 12:7), depending on what calendar you use. It's hard to interpret these figures. A simplistic approach has been to say that once 1290 days had passed and God hadn't intervened, someone then added verse 12 to give God another 45 days. However, if there was that much fluidity in the text, it's hard to see why verse 11 wasn't just adjusted. Why leave both numbers in the text? Perhaps we will never understand.

Clearer, though, is the focus on justice for individuals. So far, the concern seems to have been about 'the nation'—about how 'the people' will suffer and, in the end, be vindicated and rescued. But while it may be of some comfort to a person who dies resisting evil to know that their sacrifice has served the greater good, that individual is still unjustly dead. Wilfred Owen, in his poem 'Dulce et Decorum Est', relating to the carnage of World War I, calls the saying 'It is sweet and fitting to die for one's country' an 'old lie': it's just a waste.

In response, Daniel 12:2 speaks of resurrection—the clearest reference to it in the Old Testament. Interestingly, the verse doesn't seem to envisage a universal resurrection or universal judgment, for only 'many', not 'all', awake. The logic, it seems, is that not everyone needs justice after death. Perhaps, for some, their life experience was just. Others deserve raising up to everlasting life, while yet others deserve shame and contempt. Whatever the details of this particular way of imagining judgment after death, the point is that God will act to bring justice to individuals; he is not just concerned with the overall fate of Israel as a nation. In this context, there is also an assertion of the ultimate security of God's people: what matters is whether we are written in the book, not the vagaries of life on earth.

The final verse of the book is somehow fitting: 'But you, go your way, and rest; you shall rise for your reward at the end of the days.' It is an assertion of God's sovereignty, which in different ways has been at the heart of the book, in both the court tales and the visions. God is sovereign, so we can go on our way and rest. Justice will come ('you shall rise for your reward'), even though it may seem delayed ('at the end of the days').

Guidelines

This week we have wrestled with a style of writing that is opaque to most of us. Nevertheless, the issue at the heart of Daniel 7—12 is always with us. How do we cope with suffering? How can we believe in a good and powerful God when terrible things happen and God seems absent?

Many of us, at some time, will have experienced suffering that has caused us to question and doubt; if we have not experienced it ourselves, we will have seen it in others. In that context, we might even understand why chapters 8—12 keep on examining the same issue from different perspectives. When something terrible happens, that is what we do—revisiting it time and time again, trying to make sense of it and make our peace with it.

A number of points emerged from Daniel 7—12. First of all, we can be aware that suffering is within God's knowledge of how the world currently is. That awareness does not make the suffering less painful, yet it can help us avoid false expectations, which only add to the trauma when suffering comes. Alongside this, we hear and see others crying out 'How long?' and being made ill by their confusion and depression, and perhaps we can also hang on to their confidence that God is still sovereign and that suffering will come to an end. We have been reminded that it is a battle, within which our loyalty and dedication to God are important. Finally, God's justice does not just mean that things will be 'put right' on a large scale; it also means that every pain we suffer will not be forgotten by God.

There is no 'answer' to human suffering. There is hope in the knowledge that Jesus suffered but was resurrected, yet that is no answer to those who are undergoing suffering. Perhaps, though, something of the way Daniel tries to explore the issue may be of benefit for ourselves or for others.

Cock-crow lullaby

Many well-known Christmas carols home in on the image of the newborn child. Some are even written in the form of a lullaby, as though willing the infant Messiah to delay through slumber the day when he will discover his true and harrowing mission in the world. In parts of rural Wales, a different kind of carol singing is being rediscovered. Dating back hundreds of years, the 'plygain' or 'cock-crow' carols are so called because they were sung in the early hours of Christmas morning. An entire community would gather and, in no particular order, small groups would come forward to sing their own salvation song. The plygain typically express the whole sweep of God's redeeming work, from the garden of Eden to Galilee and beyond. The earliest texts that we have today date from the 17th century. For the most part, they are simple folk songs without any great musical or literary merit, but they do betray the influences of the William Morgan Bible (1588). Later texts were influenced by the great Methodist revivals of the 18th century. The lyrics are shot through with scriptural allusions, drawing heavily on Old Testament prophecy and apocalyptic writings.

In this set of readings, we will focus on the early chapters of the Gospels of Matthew and Luke—the two evangelists who offer us detailed, though contrasting, accounts of the nativity of Christ. Some sections will be so familiar that we can recite them. Others will be startlingly unfamiliar. At each point we are seeking a new perspective on an old story. We will set the readings alongside short extracts from plygain carols and from the more refined work of two great hymn writers, both of whom would have been steeped in the plygain tradition before they ever composed lines of their own.

Christmas sermons sometimes remind us that the infant cradled in the crib in Bethlehem will become the man lifted up on the cross at Calvary, but the connectedness of this story is more than a chronological development. This is a place of encounter where, in revisiting the words on the page, we visit the Word made flesh. As we recognise the tragedy that there is no room in our hurried lives for the Christ, we also discover the reality that, in him, there is always room for us. As we read together, may we listen for the cock-crow that will wake us to the saving presence of Christ in our lives.

These notes use the Revised Standard Version of the Bible.

1 Family history

Matthew 1:1–17

Here is our Holiday full of joy,
when Jesus Christ came as a boy.
In Bethlehem for all to see,
By oxen's stall, at Mary's knee,
Thus was opened to one and all
The place of mercy closed since Adam's fall.
The Son of God possessed the key
To open all treasure to you and me.
WELSH TRADITIONAL, DINAS MAWDDWY

Today's passage is a genealogy. At first sight it may not make gripping reading, but then again, family history has never been so popular as it is today. It may be that the phenomenon has something to do with a sense of rootlessness. In an individualistic society, I have a tendency to see myself at the very centre of things—but how did I get there? What is my deep-down identity? What is the meaning of me?

Contemporary or not, it is unlikely that you will attend a carol service this Christmas that incorporates the full nativity narrative from Matthew's Gospel—or from Luke's, for that matter. Even the most fluent of lesson readers would stumble over this list of names! In reading scripture, we constantly (and understandably) overlook genealogies. If you have ever tried to read the Old Testament right through starting from page 1, it will not have been long before you skipped one. For example, take a look at the table of nations in Genesis 10—Noah's family tree.

Matthew makes answering the 'Why?'question easy for us by setting out his answer in verse 1: 'The book of the genealogy of Jesus Christ, the son of David, the son of Abraham.' His aim is to demonstrate two truths: first, that Jesus is the fulfilment of God's promises to David, told and retold within the Jewish tradition; and second, that he is the fulfilment of

God's promise to Abraham and, through him, to the Gentiles. Matthew wants us to be blown away by the 'big picture' of God's plan. We detect a similar purpose in the mind of the anonymous composer of the plygain verse above. Jesus is the one who unlocks to us all treasures with the key of David (Revelation 3:7). He heralds a new beginning for Adam's race (Romans 5:14–15).

Have you or a member of your family ever researched your family tree? Take time to reflect on why we take such an interest in discovering our own ancestry. Tomorrow we will take a closer look at Matthew's genealogy of Jesus. What is its relevance for us today?

2 The feminine touch

Matthew 1:1–17

I will venture there in daring;
See the sceptre in his hand,
Golden pointer for the sinner
Full acceptance—all can stand.
ANN GRIFFITHS (1776–1805)

Every family has at least one black sheep and, looking closely at this lineage, we find the makings of a small flock. Take the women, for instance. Apart from Mary, we learn of Tamar, Rahab, Ruth and Bathsheba (referred to in verses 6–7 as the mother of Solomon and wife of Uriah). Tamar passed herself off as a prostitute; Rahab was one. Bathsheba committed adultery with David, and Ruth was a foreigner (as, of course, was Rahab). Yet each, in her own way, showed courage, each had a part to play and each influenced the course of history. Perhaps that is why they are included here.

There are many more surprises in this genealogy. The Messiah's ancestry is traced via Joseph—famous foster father, but not a blood relation—and the descent is not always by way of the firstborn son. We hear of Isaac's second son, Jacob, and not his firstborn, Esau. In the case of Jacob, it is not his first, second or third son, but the fourth, Judah, who continues the line. In blessing Judah, Jacob promised that 'the sceptre shall not depart from Judah, nor the ruler's staff from between his feet, until he comes to whom it belongs' (Genesis 49:10). It is this fourth son's descendant who will be the Messiah-king, holding the sceptre as ruler of all the nations (see Psalm 2:7–9).

Ann Griffiths is another unlikely woman who deserves a place of note in history. She ranks among the greatest of Welsh poets and hymn writers, yet she never wrote down her work. She died in childbirth at the age of 29 and might have remained obscure and unread were it not for the fact that her verses were learned and passed on by her companion, Ruth. In the lines quoted above, and in the imagery she chooses, Ann offers us a new way into the Christmas story. In ancient times, the sign of the sceptre could instil great dread (see Esther 4:9—5:3). Ann Griffiths understands that the incarnation is not about our reaching out to gather a helpless infant into our arms. Rather, it is about none other than the Godhead reaching out in welcome to us. Where we might have expected destruction, here is embrace. This is no stand-alone crib scene. It is the outworking of the oldest, greatest and most unlikely promise known to humankind. Matthew's Christmas list may not make for the most exciting of reading, but its implications are immense.

3 Joseph's dreams

Matthew 1:18–25

All poor men and humble, all lame men who stumble,
Come, haste ye, nor feel ye afraid,
For Jesus, our treasure, with love past all measure,
In lowly poor manger was laid.
K.E. ROBERTS (1877–1962)

It is important to note that the passage we have read today takes up where the genealogy leaves off. This is a link that we overlook every time we wheel out our Matthew–Luke conflated nativity story, commencing with the appearance of the angel in Joseph's dream or at Mary's door.

Matthew seeks to capture our attention with an unexpected ending. He has not written, 'Jacob the father of Joseph, the father of Jesus', as the listener might have expected, but 'Jacob the father of Joseph the husband of Mary, of whom Jesus was born, who is called Christ' (1:16). Strange genealogy indeed! This is why Matthew needs to explain in detail how the birth of Jesus came about.

He introduces Joseph. Of course we know all about the first Joseph, and how his brothers styled him (Genesis 37:19), but have we noticed that Matthew records no fewer than four occasions on which the New Testament Joseph receives instruction or guidance in a dream? We have no account of his background or childhood, and certainly there is no indication that he employed a special dream gift as a means of gloating over his siblings, but Matthew does seem to want to draw some parallels with the famous Genesis story. Later on (2:14), we will hear of Joseph going down to Egypt—the only New Testament man to do so. Like the other Joseph, he has a father named Jacob. Like the other Joseph, he is entrusted with great responsibility and proves himself equal to the task.

So what of the first dream and its consequence? Mary is found to be with child 'of the Holy Spirit' (v. 18). The angel of the Lord is recorded as speaking to 'Joseph, son of David' (v. 20). Matthew demonstrates that Jesus is both Son of God and Son of David, fulfilment of promise and hope of the world (see 2 Samuel 7:8–17; Romans 1:3–4). In due course, Joseph will respond in obedience by doing two things. He will take Mary home as his wife, indicating that he assumes responsibility for her and for the child she will bear. The second and more radical step will be to adopt the child as his own by giving him a name—Jesus.

We have heard edited highlights from the nativity story on so many occasions that we may have assumed a certain perspective on the sequence of events. You might like to take time today to meditate on the first chapter of Matthew's Gospel as a whole and make a note of any new insights you have gained.

4 Broad canvas

This thy beauty will not tarnish,
Ever freshly kindled flame,
Through all ages, time eternal,
Never tiring, peerless same.
WILLIAM WILLIAMS, PANTYCELYN (1717–91)

This narrative has a careful structure. We begin to recognise the sequence of event and instruction, reference to the prophet and prophecy fulfilled. There are at least five Old Testament quotations in these two chapters. Yesterday we read (in Matthew 1:23) the Immanuel saying from Isaiah 7:14. Today we are reminded of Micah's reference to Bethlehem (Micah 5:2) and of a promise made by the Lord to David: 'You shall be prince over Israel' (2 Samuel 5:2).

This passage has given rise to endless deliberations. Were the magi astronomers or astrologers, priests or magicians? Did they come from Persia or Babylon, Arabia or Syria? And what of the 'star in the east'? The great astronomer Kepler suggested that it might have been a planetary conjunction of Jupiter, Saturn and Mars. Could it have been a comet? Halley's comet would have been visible in 12–11BC. Or was it a supernova, a new star, which can for a time shine even brighter than the moon?

These discussions are intriguing and may yield yet more food for thought, but the Gospels are not and were never meant to be dispassionate historical narrative. Attempts to deconstruct and reconstruct them as such are doomed to fail. As we have begun to see, Matthew's detail is intended to help us expand our appreciation of salvation's story and not limit it. If chapter 1 is painted on a broad canvas, today's instalment is intended to develop our understanding still further. In this child, all God's promises are fulfilled.

The real question for us is whether we will share the joy of the magi. Matthew does not speak of the shepherds. We will have to wait for Luke, before we can learn of their significance. For Matthew, the first visitors to bow down and worship are Gentiles, foreigners. The newborn baby is

Abraham's son, through whom all nations of the world are to be blessed (Genesis 22:18).

5 Good king, bad king

On this day's morn, a little child, a little child,
The root of Jesse was born, a little child,
The Mighty One of Bozra,
The Lawgiver on Mount Sinai,
The Atonement won on Calvary, a little child, a little child,
Sucking at Mary's breast, a little child.
WELSH TRADITIONAL

In the previous scene, we heard mention of two kings. King Herod had the advantage of the Jewish scriptures and all the wise advisers Jerusalem could offer, but he failed even to approach the insight of the foreign magi, who had discovered much through their observations of the created world (see Romans 1:20). The new king of the Jews is as yet an infant, but it is to him that both created world and prophetic word seem to point.

Today's instalment sees the holy family flee Israel and escape to Egypt. Thanks to the Lord's warning to Joseph in another dream, they outwit Herod's terrible command. This is a strange and frightening passage of scripture and we may find ourselves asking why Herod was unable, in such a small town, to locate a very unusual family with a young baby who had already played host to a group of exotic visitors from the east.

By now familiar with Matthew's storytelling style, we cannot help but hear in this narrative an echo of another great hero of the past. Moses was God's chosen instrument to lead his people from slavery to freedom. As an infant, he too was in grave danger because of the cruel edict of a tyrant king (Exodus 1:15–22). Matthew is writing of the new Moses, who comes to set all peoples free. At this point the fulfilment game can feel very convoluted. Why was it necessary in God's grand scheme that the Ramah prophecy should come to pass (Jeremiah 31:15)? Perhaps the answer is found in the sheer fury and irrationality of an evil king. As the saying goes (attributed to Lord Acton), 'power tends to corrupt and absolute power corrupts absolutely'. King Herod chose not to seek out one child but to use his power to order the destruction of all.

Joseph is no head-in-the-clouds dreamer. Time and again he recognises the Lord's guidance in his life. Then he obeys and eludes a further series of dangers. After Herod's death he is able to take the family back to Israel, but has to avoid Judea, where another tyrant king has succeeded to the throne. The family settles in Nazareth, a place of no great reputation (John 1:46), but somehow this fulfils a prophecy too (v. 23).

6 Lost for words

Luke 1:5–25

Let us consider the love of the Trinity, freely willed, freely willed,
In setting out a way of covenant, freely willed;
The Father chose the surety,
The Son was content to suffer;
The Holy Spirit gave his gifts, freely willed, freely willed,
To bring Zion home, freely willed.
WELSH TRADITIONAL

If a first observation about the way we approach Matthew's nativity narrative is that we tend to forget about the genealogy, a first observation regarding Luke's presentation might be that we overlook the place of John the Baptist. In the first few chapters, Luke seems to speak of him just as much as he does of Jesus. Only after we have listened to the annunciation of Elizabeth's pregnancy do we hear of the angel's visit to Mary. Only after we have listened to a description of John's birth do we hear the parallel account for Jesus.

What, then, is the role of John? There is certainly a link between his story and the Old Testament story of Samuel. Elkanah and Hannah had waited a long time for a child, and, when the child did arrive, he was dedicated to the service of God (1 Samuel 1:27–28). In addition, although John denies outright that he is Elijah come back to life (John 1:21), he stands in this prophetic tradition also. The angel tells Zechariah that John will go forth 'in the spirit and power of Elijah' (Luke 1:17). His clothes will resemble those of the prophet, and John too will challenge kings (his confrontation with Herod and Herodias in Matthew 14 recalls Elijah's dealings with Ahab and Jezebel in 1 Kings 18).

Elizabeth and Zechariah are described as 'righteous before God' (1:6). They were not only advanced in years but were also of great spiritual maturity. Their sorrow was their childlessness, but perhaps this very experience of hardship had been to them a source of growth. Enter the angel with the news they have always longed for but which, by now, they scarcely hope to hear. Zechariah understandably cross-examines the angel and is chastised for his lack of faith—but surely this loss of words is more of a sign than a punishment. It is Zechariah's inability to speak that makes the people realise that something extraordinary has taken place.

Is there a particular sorrow for you at this time? We may not be able to answer the question of why we should face difficulties or disappointments in our lives, but we can cry out to the one who is big enough to hold our pain. Elizabeth and Zechariah were content, in the words of St David, to 'keep the faith and do the little things'. Inspired by today's reading, may we ask for God's strength to do the same.

Guidelines

What is the Christmas story? It may be that, after this week's readings, the question does not sound quite so straightforward as it would have done before. Spend a few minutes reflecting on your response. Do you think your answer is primarily influenced by your reading of Matthew, Luke or other parts of scripture—for example, the prophetic writings, the first chapter of John's Gospel, or what we learn of Jesus' family and the society of his day through the accounts of his later public ministry? Or are there unexpected sources that have defined your understanding—a story heard, a favourite poem or painting, a particular film, or even the nativity play at school? As in the accounts of Matthew and Luke, each re-telling will have a particular slant or message to convey. Spend time giving thanks to God for this wealth of different perspectives and ask him how they can be ways in, for you, to a deeper awareness of salvation's song.

You might want to seek out someone else with whom to explore this question. Consider whether you could take a break from the last-minute preparations this week to encounter the message of the nativity in a new way. Could you pause from the shopping for an hour to call into a local art gallery, or put your feet up with a DVD? If you are someone for whom these days mean an endless round of carol services and concerts, look out for the ways in which these retellings try to harmonise the narratives of Matthew and Luke. How does the familiar become a reawakening? Allow yourself to be drawn into the reality that is Emmanuel.

1 Angels and prophets

Luke 1:26–38

An order was opened through freely granted love
Flowing outward like a fountain
Of grace, with gifts for the race of mankind
From the bosom of God himself.
WELSH TRADITIONAL

Having told the story of the annunciation of John's birth, Luke now presents us with the parallel account for Jesus. Some details are constant, some dramatically different. John is the support act, Jesus the one for whom they have waited all along.

In promising John's birth, the angel is bringing the Lord's answer to the anguished prayers of Zechariah and Elizabeth over many years. Mary, on the other hand, is still young and unmarried—and yet, in Gabriel's words to Mary, we find an unbroken word of promise echoing back through the years. 'He will be great, and will be called the Son of the Most High; and the Lord God will give to him the throne of his father David, and he will reign over the house of Jacob for ever; and of his kingdom there will be no end' (vv. 32–33). The name, the throne, the kingdom: all these features recall the words of the prophet Nathan to David in 2

Samuel 7. As we have seen, Matthew too identifies the link with David. This moment has been in the making for a long, long time.

We have already heard of the deep piety of Zechariah and Elizabeth. We might almost ask ourselves why it was not Elizabeth, in her maturity, who was chosen to be the mother of Jesus. For Mary, the 'gift' was unsought and unexpected. What was critical in her case was not that she had always hoped for a child but that she chose to accept what Gabriel proclaimed. Zechariah needed to believe that it was still possible for Elizabeth, at her time in life, to bear a child. Mary needed to accept a far greater miracle than that—and she did: 'Let it be to me according to your word' (v. 38).

'An order was opened through freely granted love...' Mary can have had no idea of the extent of the love of which she, in her availability, became a part. Take a moment to reflect on your plans and priorities. Are they more about what you think God might be able to do through you than about availability to being transformed by his love?

2 Mothers' song

Luke 1:39–56

Here is the tent of meeting,
Here is the life redeemed,
Here is the sinner welcomed,
Here is the sufferer healed.
ANN GRIFFITHS

Just as Gabriel made a sign of Zechariah in his silence, a sign is given to Mary that the birth of Jesus will come to pass. Elizabeth is pregnant. She has remained in seclusion these last five months (1:24) and so, through the angel's words, Mary is among the first to know. She hurries to her relative's home, and Elizabeth and her unborn child prophesy the arrival of the mother of their Lord. This strange detail of the communication from the womb is not without precedent in scripture. In a different kind of prophetic act, we hear that Rebekah's babies 'jostled each other within her' (Genesis 25:22–23, NIV), as an indication of the warring between Jacob and Esau that was to come.

Luke's writings always give a special place to the women who followed the Messiah, and in this scene we might say that we have a portrait of the first two disciples of Jesus. Elizabeth's insight is extraordinary and, in her words to Mary, she displays eyes of faith and a way of blessing that Jesus will speak of a long time hence (v. 45; see John 20:29).

Mary's song is stunning and contains within it echoes of Isaiah 61, a passage that reverberates throughout the Gospel of Luke: good news for the poor and the hungry, for the humble and the oppressed. These are more than words. They are a way in to the greater mystery of Christ's presence. Ann Griffiths' hymn, quoted above, speaks of the same kind of good news. She draws on the Old Testament imagery of a tent of meeting or tabernacle. But ultimately this is neither a temporary shelter nor a building. It is not so much about a physical space as a moment of encounter. Ann speaks with disarming simplicity of the quiet meeting place with God. Take time to read Mary's song again. What is there in your experience that resonates with the hymn she shares?

3 Firstborn

Luke 1:57–80

The Daniel's true Messiah on Mary's knee,
The wise child of Isaiah,
The promise given to Adam,
The Alpha and Omega, on Mary's knee, on Mary's knee,
In a stall in Bethlehem Judah, on Mary's knee.
WELSH TRADITIONAL

A feature that all the plygain carols share is that they are not the songs of an individual but of a community. When Zechariah sings his song at the birth of John, he also expresses the joy of his people at the goodness of their God.

Jesus himself will affirm the significance of John the Baptist: he is both a prophet and more than a prophet. 'Among those born of women,' says

Jesus, 'none is greater than John' (Luke 7:26–28), and yet John heralds both the beginning and the end of an era. John teaches the Law and the Prophets. Jesus brings the good news of the kingdom (16:16). John is indeed the long-awaited child for Elizabeth and Zechariah, but he is also a gift to all people. We read that when Elizabeth gave birth, all the neighbours and relatives heard of the Lord's mercy 'and they rejoiced with her' (1:58). Of course there were months of waiting before Zechariah declared John's name and his tongue was loosed. Once started, though, there was no stopping him, as he gave voice to a prophetic hymn of praise that we still sing today.

Once again, there is recourse to a whole series of Old Testament scriptures: the promises to Abraham and David, Isaiah's words of hope, Malachi's talk of the Lord's messenger (see Genesis 26:3; Psalm 132:16–17; Isaiah 40:3; Malachi 3:1), and so on and on. It is possible to take Zechariah's song to pieces, to analyse which phrase draws on which scripture, which words are recalled verbatim and which are found to differ from the texts that we have received. This can be a worthwhile exercise, and yet we must take care. Zechariah's prophecy is, above all, an exuberant hymn of praise. The best way to appreciate its meaning is to raise our voices and join in.

4 House of bread

Luke 2:1–20

'What a thrill it was to attend the parish church at Llanllyfni for the carol service at five o'clock in the morning! We tramped there together in crowds, all denominational pride gone and all arguments forgotten. Were we not on the way to Bethlehem? I remember the shadows lingering in the corners of the old church, and the sons of the sexton singing like the angels of God.'
REMINISCENCE FROM LLANLLYFNI, CAERMARTHENSHIRE, C.1910

Today we arrive at Luke's account of the birth of Jesus. Why is it that we hear this passage solely at Christmas time, and then only as an excerpt from the narrative in which it is set? For Luke, this is no isolated event. Rather, it is intricately woven into the fabric of the story he tells—a story of encounter, transformation and praise. Time and again in the third Gospel and the book of Acts, we hear of people caught up in wonder, amazement and awe. This, for Luke, is the impact of the narrative he must relate. 'And the shepherds returned, glorifying and praising God for all they had heard and seen' (v. 20).

So, as we look afresh at Luke's account of the nativity, we see his awareness of promise fulfilled, particularly in relation to the prophecies of Isaiah. Some of the links are obvious; some are less evident, suggesting to us that Luke was consciously or unconsciously thinking of the prophet as he wrote. The angel brings good news of great joy: 'To you is born this day in the city of David a Saviour, who is Christ the Lord' (v. 11): is this a reference to the glad tidings of Isaiah 61 and to the promised child of Isaiah 9? Then there is some unlikely detail, which we may overlook because we are so familiar with its depiction on our Christmas cards and nativity scenes. Luke tells us no less than three times that Jesus was lying in a manger (vv. 7, 12, 16). Is this merely to stress the humility of the Saviour's birth, or is there yet another link with Isaiah in the background: 'The ox knows his master, the donkey his owner's manger, but Israel does not know, my people do not understand' (Isaiah 1:3, NIV)? Will God's own people understand the identity of the Messiah-king?

5 Temple presence

Luke 2:21–52

Nor ere the world found shape, or heaven might,
Before the sun or moon or star shed light,
There was by Three in One designed
A saving way for helpless humankind.
WILLIAM WILLIAMS, PANTYCELYN (1717–91)

The circumcision and naming of Jesus are summarised here in very few words (v. 21), presumably included by Luke as a parallel to the equivalent events for John, which we find in 1:57–66. And yet, unlike Matthew, Luke has introduced the name of Jesus without any definition (compare v. 21 with Matthew 1:21). Is the whole of the presentation narrative his commentary on the name Jesus, perhaps—culminating as it does in the great proclamation of Simeon, 'For mine eyes have seen thy salvation, which thou hast prepared in the presence of all peoples' (vv. 30–31)?

We read on to the single event that is recorded from Jesus' later childhood (vv. 41–52). Again, the setting is the temple. Again, the people who are present are amazed at what takes place (v. 47). Once again, Mary treasures all these things in her heart (v. 51; see 2:19). Finally we read that 'Jesus increased in wisdom and stature, and in favour with God and man' (v. 52). We cannot but recall the few short verses of a further temple incident in Luke 19:45–48. Do you sense the love and agony of the one who sees his father's house transformed into a den for thieves?

What kind of waiting has this Advent season been for you? Has it flashed by in a whirl of activity and preparation? Or has each day been your own experience of agony as you seek to cope with the problems that life brings? Do your struggles involve coping with getting older, finding a sense of purpose in a particular season of your life?

We do not learn what physical limitations Simeon and Anna had to contend with, but we do learn of their passion for God's presence, their insight and their devotion to the Lord. Both were deeply aware that while there was yet breath in them, God had a purpose for their lives. Simeon and Anna were contemplatives: they were 'in the temple', for that is the literal derivation of the word. We are all called to contemplation, to be people who seek the quiet place with God, but perhaps this is a special call for you just now. Ask for the grace to respond, and look out for a Simeon or Anna—limited, perhaps, in action but able to remind you that God has a purpose for you, every day of your life.

6 Yet more names!

Luke 3:21–37

Wonder, wonder for the angels,
wonderful to eyes of faith,
to see the giver of existence,
gracious sustainer and ruler of all,
wrapped in cloths and in a manger,
without a place to lay his head,
and yet around, the host of glory,
come to worship at his birth.
ANN GRIFFITHS

The Advent waiting is played out. Today we arrive at Christmas Eve and celebrate with… yet another list of names! We have come full circle from our first reading in the Gospels two weeks ago.

There are some familiar features in Luke's genealogy. Like Matthew, he traces the ancestors through Joseph's line. By contrast, though, he works backwards, and, rather than stopping at Abraham, he continues the family tree all the way to Adam, 'the son of God'. Luke sets this passage alongside the baptism of Jesus—for, after all, it is at his baptism that Jesus is declared by God himself to be 'my beloved Son' (v. 22).

Having worked our way right through the early chapters of Matthew and Luke, it is evident once again that in neither narrative is the birth of Jesus a stand-alone scene that can be lifted out of the pages and pasted on to a greetings card. Regardless of which Gospel we are reading, we find that, as we are drawn inwards by the detail, we are also pointed outwards to the story that makes sense of it all. Matthew's writing is steeped in the Old Testament promises and the heroes of the past, in whose stories we detect the pattern of fulfilment yet to come. Luke combines his reflections on scripture with introductions to key figures like Zechariah and Elizabeth, Joseph, Mary and John, each one surprised by tidings of overwhelming joy.

Both Matthew and Luke invite us to be part of the story. They have constructed their narrative so carefully that each detail is intricately connected with another: at each twist or turn of the tale, we can recognise their overarching themes. We begin and end with genealogy, not of interest in itself, perhaps. Yet the more we, like the evangelists, become immersed in the story, the more a single name or single word will point us towards the whole.

Guidelines

Take time to reflect on these readings from Matthew and Luke. Is there a detail of the nativity narrative that has spoken to you in a fresh way, or a line from one of the carols that you would like to hold on to in the days to come? It may come as a surprise to discover that the song of salvation has been passed down to us in so many different ways. Matthew and Luke drew on an oral tradition in putting together their Gospels, as did the plygain composers in creating their popular carols. Do you think that, while rightly valuing the written word, we have lost sight of some of the other ways that we can connect with God's story in our lives? If you are involved in Christian ministry, have you explored folk traditions from your area or even from another part of the world, which may provide fresh channels for celebrating the great Christian festivals and an invitation into a life of praise?

O to have faith
to explore with the angels
the plan of salvation,
the mystery within it,
two natures, one God,
purity without confusion,
perfect through and through.
ANN GRIFFITHS

FURTHER READING

A.M. Allchin, *Praise Above All* (University of Wales Press, 1991).

Raymond E. Brown, *The Birth of the Messiah* (Doubleday, 1999).

Gwynfryn Richards, 'Y Plygain', *Journal of the Historical Society of the Church in Wales* (1947).

Haggai

Haggai is a refreshingly straightforward little book, brief and precisely dated within a single year, 520BC. The Babylonian empire has been defeated, and Persia is now in control under its ruler, Darius. His predecessor, the notable Cyrus of Isaiah 44:28 and 45:1, pursued the enlightened policy of returning exiled peoples to their homelands: hence Israel's return from exile in 538BC. But now, only a few years later, life is not what they expected. Disillusionment has set in—a weary apathy—and it is to this situation that Haggai speaks.

His main concern is the rebuilding of the temple, now in ruins, and the restoration of worship at the heart of the community. In this he is often compared unfavourably with the great pre-exilic prophets such as Isaiah and Amos. They were uninhibited in condemning the state of the nation's worship at the time: through them God said, 'I have had enough of burnt offerings... I am weary' (Isaiah 1:11–14); 'I hate, I despise your festivals... but let justice roll down like waters' (Amos 5:21–24). What use were elaborate rituals without commitment to justice for the needy and rescue for the oppressed? Such were the priorities of Israel's God.

Now, though, times have changed. The returned exiles are a small, struggling community in a hostile world. There are no elaborate rituals now. It is more a question of keeping worship alive, of maintaining their distinctive faith and putting God first in their reckoning, affirming him as Lord.

Contrasted with those of Isaiah and Amos, Haggai's concerns may seem narrow and restricted, focused on a particular moment in history and the needs of a small community. Yet such is the power of God's living, active word that this brief message, addressed to a situation many centuries ago, can still challenge us in our world today to examine our priorities and resolve to put God first.

These notes are based mainly on the New Revised Standard Version of the Bible.

1 An economy in trouble

Haggai 1:1–6

Everything seemed to have gone wrong. The community was reestablished in its homeland after years of exile in Babylon, but reality fell far short of their hopes. Where was the joy and exuberant delight envisaged by that great prophet-poet of the exile (Isaiah 55:12)? They were dissatisfied and disillusioned.

Haggai's challenge is direct and uncomfortable. Their priorities are wrong. Food and shelter were immediate necessities as they reestablished themselves, but now luxury has crept in. Preoccupied with their well-built, panelled houses, they have had no time to restore the ruins of God's house, their central place of worship, the temple. Haggai's advice is practical. Take stock, look at the problems—at all that effort with little achievement—and, in a memorable phrase, think about why you 'earn wages to put them into a bag with holes' (v. 6)! Know the feeling?

Haggai has an answer. Stop procrastinating, saying, 'The time has not yet come to rebuild the Lord's house' (v. 2). Put God first, and make sure that commitment has visible expression at the heart of the community's life. The challenge comes with the authority of the Lord of hosts ('the Lord Almighty', NIV)—Haggai's preferred title for God, which he frequently repeats. His God has the power to make things different.

Apathy, by its nature, creeps in undetected, and procrastination is often tempting. There are so many things to do in a busy life: 'the time has not yet come...' But God's time is always 'now'. That's why another prophet pleads urgently, 'Seek the Lord while he may be found; call on him while he is near', with the promise to follow: 'You will go out in joy and be led forth in peace' (Isaiah 55:6, 12, NIV).

2 The road to recovery

Haggai 1:7–11

Haggai's challenge is urgent and intensely practical. Recognise the past for what it is (literally 'set your mind on it') and then get to work—in this case, hard manual work. Wallowing in self-pity and regret for what has gone by is simply a recipe for depression, but resolve and determination for a better future bring renewal and hope. Haggai sees in a restored temple a symbol of fresh commitment and devotion to the Lord, and, more than that, the promise of a glimpse of divine glory (v. 8: 'that I may appear in my glory', RSV).

Haggai was a man of his time, speaking in the thought-forms of that pre-scientific age two and a half millennia ago. It is too easy for us, with our more sophisticated scientific awareness, to write off the continuing relevance of ancient prophets such as this one. Catastrophes in the natural world are not a sign of judgment on those who suffer, though we have come to recognise that, for some such disasters, we ourselves may be accountable: there is a moral responsibility. To be fair, the Old Testament itself does not automatically make a simplistic connection between natural disaster and divine judgment, as a glance at the final song of Habakkuk (an earlier prophet than Haggai) makes clear. In triumphant faith, Habakkuk declares that although famine may come and disaster be heaped on disaster, 'yet I will rejoice in the Lord' (Habakkuk 3:18).

Haggai is not a prophet of doom. His scathing strictures on his contemporaries are a word of hope. Haggai's God is a transforming, patient, saving God. The community that sets worship at its heart has a future as a strengthened, unified people—and the visible symbol of that worship and of their resolve to put God first is to be the restored temple, affirming their identity as the people of Yahweh. Make no mistake, however: nowhere in the Old Testament is the temple regarded as any more than the focus of God's earthly presence. Let Solomon's moving words in his prayer of dedication of the temple lift up our hearts in praise: 'Will God indeed dwell on the earth? Even heaven and the highest heaven cannot contain you, much less this house that I have built!' (1 Kings 8:27).

3 From apathy to action

How many Christians would include Haggai as one of their favourite books of the Bible? It is short enough to be easily overlooked, and its inclusion among the 'Minor Prophets' (disparagingly so called nowadays) is hardly enticing. Yet what treasures there are, waiting to be discovered in these ancient scriptures! Today's short passage is packed with food for thought and material for prayer and reflection.

What enabled the community's transformation from apathy to action? First, they 'obeyed the voice of the Lord their God' (v. 12)—and this obedience came not just from the two leaders (Zerubbabel, his name implying perhaps that he was born in exile, and Joshua) but from 'all the remnant of the people'. 'Remnant' is an interesting word. In everyday language it indicates something left over, primarily of cloth—a cheap bargain. But here in Haggai it describes the small community of returned exiles, a reminder that God is not defeated. In the face of apathy, indifference and hostile forces, come what may, there is always hope for the future. God does not leave himself without a witness. There is always a 'remnant' bearing the seed of hope.

And here is democracy, equality before the Lord! Again, it is not just the two leaders who are inspired by the Lord and cajole the people, but 'the Lord stirred up the spirit' of all the people (v. 14). The leaders were not intermediaries between the people and God. They were all inspired together, and all cooperating. Nor was there just human determination involved, but divine inspiration—God himself at work and everyone responsive to the Lord.

However, none of this would have happened without the faithful commitment of one man, Haggai, not because of his foresight or superior gifts of his own but because he was 'sent' by God (v. 12) (the Hebrew word used here is equivalent to the Greek word from which 'apostle' comes). Such were his credentials: the Lord's messenger speaking the Lord's message. Here was the secret of his success. And the heart of that message was, 'I am with you, says the Lord' (v. 13). Work began that day on the temple that lasted until it was destroyed by the Roman general Pompey in 63BC.

Still today God's word has power to transform a situation when faithfully delivered by his messengers.

4 The future belongs to God

Haggai 2:1–9

The rebuilding has begun, but some of the people feel only disappointment. This house of God is small-scale compared with Solomon's majestic temple. Yet this too is a perpetual reminder of God's presence among them and of their obligation to worship. Again there is an inclusive note—everyone, people as well as leaders, is called to action—and the ground of their courage is God's promise, 'I am with you' (v. 4). This is a personal relationship: 'I and you'. Still today it is confidence in his presence with us that must undergird our actions.

There's a reminder here of two possible attitudes to past history: one is a nostalgic, dead-end regret for a past that was seemingly greater than the present; the other is the memory of God's past mercies as the assurance of future blessing, for God is unchanging, 'the same yesterday, today and for ever' (Hebrews 13:8). Israel, even as Haggai spoke, was commemorating the exodus from Egypt in the annual Feast of Tabernacles/Booths (v. 1; compare Leviticus 23:39–43). We, too, commemorate God's saving action in his victory over death and sin by the life-giving power of the cross.

Inevitably, in reading this ancient text, written in a language vastly different from ours, we come up against problems and limitations of translation. In today's passage there are two important theological words: *cabod* ('glory') and *shalom* ('peace'). How best to translate them? A glance at two or more English versions illustrates the point. 'I will fill this house with splendour', says verse 7 in the NRSV; contrast NIV 'with glory', a word associated with God's presence (1 Kings 8:10–11). Then, verse 9 says, 'And I will give prosperity' (NRSV); contrast 'peace' (NIV), a word indicating far more than 'prosperity'.

Haggai is a visionary; in faith he sees beyond the immediate. Can we match his faith, recognising God's glory in the cross (John 17:1) and the reality of his peace in our lives and worship?

5 How is holiness acquired?

Haggai 2:10–19

The splendid vision of God's future is one thing, the response of the people quite another. They have set to work restoring the temple, but outward compliance is not enough, says Haggai. What counts is genuine commitment to the Lord. Despite all their efforts, what they offer is unclean (v. 14). They must have felt as if God was never satisfied.

This time, the message is addressed directly to the priests, the experts in legal niceties who can give an authoritative ruling (*torah*) on a point of law. How is holiness acquired? Is it transmitted simply by contact with what is sacred, or does it demand the deep inner commitment of those who worship? Haggai's illustration strikes us as a strange, abstruse point, but, put in terms of health and disease, it is immediately more meaningful. Haggai is asking an uncomfortably searching question: how genuine is their devotion to the Lord, how life-changing their commitment? Worship was being reinstated with its holy rituals. Could that, of itself, confer holiness on the worshippers?

The second part of his question is equally significant and its answer is beyond dispute. Even the holy offerings were rendered unacceptable by the uncleanness of the worshippers.

As I suggested in the Introduction to these notes, Haggai is sometimes unfairly compared with the great pre-exilic prophets, as being too narrowly concerned with the rituals and ceremonies of worship. But he knows that spiritual commitment finds its expression in worship, and the rebuilt temple is the visible evidence of that commitment at the heart of the community. To suppose that God responds to outward observances, without the spiritual transformation of the worshippers, is a denial of his nature as the God who calls his people into covenant relationship with himself. What was needed was a change of heart.

Today's reading ends on a high note. With God there is always a future, with new possibilities blotting out past failure. Even in Haggai's stern words of rebuke there is the seed of hope: 'From this day on I will bless you' (v. 19).

6 The Messiah foreshadowed

Haggai 2:20–23

At first sight, this final section of Haggai seems a let-down—a sadly negative, abrupt ending to a prophet who has given so much to challenge and encourage us. Here, earthly kingdoms and all their trappings of power are to be overthrown in a cosmic upheaval. Those who have lived by the sword will die by the sword. Haggai is not speaking in literal, historical terms of disturbance within the Persian empire, but rather of God's action on a grander scale against all that opposes his rule (v. 22). Amid the wreckage of earth's empires, God's power stands supreme.

After the return from exile, high hopes rested on Zerubbabel, a descendant of David's royal line. He is described here in messianic terms as God's chosen one, acting with divine authority, just as the king's signet conferred royal authority as truly as if the king himself were present. But Zerubbabel soon disappeared from history, the ending of his story unknown to us. Haggai's vision was necessarily timebound, relating to a particular moment in history, but its ultimate fulfilment awaited another royal Son of David's house—the Messiah, who was destined to fulfil another prophet's different vision, that of the suffering servant 'wounded for our transgressions, crushed for our iniquities' (Isaiah 53:5). If ever there was a 'shaking of heaven and earth', surely it was at that moment of desolation on the cross and at the final triumph of the dying Saviour: 'It is finished!' (John 19:30).

Don't look for strict logic in Haggai, determined by human reason. Rather, he portrays the future in impressionistic terms, foreshortened and later to be reinterpreted with regard to a greater Servant. But whatever Haggai's limitations, this is to his credit: his God is never too small, but the Lord Almighty who seeks us as his worshippers today.

'O God, whose beauty is beyond our imagining and whose power we cannot comprehend, show us your glory as far as we can grasp it, and shield us from knowing more than we can bear until we may look upon you without fear, through Jesus Christ our Saviour.'
Post-Communion Prayer for the Third Sunday after Trinity

Guidelines

An ancient text like Haggai makes particular demands on us who read it as Christians today. His prescientific worldview, his apparently un-questioning link between natural disaster and divine judgment, and his different culture dig a gulf between us. Yet we must avoid the temptation to read this book only as ancient history or literature, irrelevant to our modern times. As holy scripture, it brings an uncomfortable challenge to our faith and commitment in our equally insecure and troubled world. Are my priorities right in balancing material concerns with the spiritual dimension?

FURTHER READING

J. Baldwin, Haggai, *Zechariah, Malachi* (Tyndale Old Testament Commentary) (IVP, 1972).

R. Mason, *The Books of Haggai, Zechariah and Malachi* (Cambridge Bible Commentaries) (CUP, 1977).

This page is intentionally left blank.

The BRF

Magazine

Richard Fisher writes...

What does 'discipleship' mean to you? I remember talking with someone a few years ago about BRF's work in this area. He was a Christian, very actively involved in his own church. He express surprise that we used the term 'discipleship' at all. His view was that most people didn't understand what it meant and would be put off by it. It quickly became clear that he didn't understand what it meant himself.

At the end of Matthew's Gospel Jesus gives his disciples a command that has become known as the Great Commission: 'Go and make disciples of all nations...' As Christians, and as the Church, we should be in the business of making disciples. Making disciples is about encouraging, resourcing and equipping people to follow Jesus Christ, to discern his call on their lives and to serve him to the best of their ability, in whatever circumstances they find themselves. It's an ongoing process that will last a lifetime.

It's a process that we all should be engaged in, whether we've been a Christian for five minutes or for decades. I wonder how much emphasis your church places on discipleship. Is it talked about much? How much attention do you give it yourself? The problem is that it takes time. I've talked to many people about this, especially since *Foundations21* (BRF's web-based discipleship resource) first became available. They've told me that while they admire what we're trying to resource through *Foundations21*, the main challenge is getting people to see that developing their own Christian understanding and then actually putting it into practice is important and worth investing time and energy in.

Discipleship is something we at BRF are passionate about! If you like using a computer, why not try out *Foundations21*? If you prefer books, take a look at some of our publications. Whether on the web or on paper, we'd like to think we have something to offer you in your journey of discipleship. In his classic book *Discipleship*, first printed in 1981, David Watson wrote, 'I have a growing conviction that Discipleship is one of the vital issues for today.' Thirty years later, I believe it still is.

To register free with Foundations21, go to www.foundations21.net
For BRF discipleship publications, go to www.brfonline.org.uk

Facing the Darkness and Finding the Light

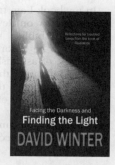

David Winter

Most people think of Revelation, that strange book of visions that ends the New Testament, as bewildering and rather terrifying. Apart from a few familiar verses, such as 'Behold, I stand at the door and knock' (3:20), and the great vision of peace and joy in the new Jerusalem with which it ends, it's generally regarded as a book best left to the 'experts'. Much of it is violent and ugly—horses up to their haunches in blood, giant green locusts swarming from bottomless pits, sundry horrific monsters, the dreaded 'four horsemen of the Apocalypse' and so on—so why should anyone *choose* to read it?

Yet Revelation is part of the Christian scriptures, and '*all* scripture is inspired by God' (2 Timothy 3:16). Among these visions of horror, there is a sacred message—in fact, as I would argue, a message of hope exactly tuned to the needs of an age like ours. These visions were given to people like us who were anxious and apprehensive, unable to make sense of much that was going on around them, fearful that secular power and godless evil would overwhelm them. The vivid pictures seen by the seer John were not given to terrify but to reassure.

Revelation is not an 'easy read', of course. At times it's distinctly scary. We don't overcome our fears, however, by pretending they don't exist, but by facing them. In Revelation we are forced to look evil in the face, to identify motives and actions that are contrary to the will of God, but we are also offered, all the while, an alternative vision. Each picture of horror and evil is matched by a visit to what I call the 'heavenly throne room', where God and 'the Lamb', Jesus, are seated, surrounded by the saints and angels pouring out their prayers and worship. This, not the courts of Rome or the great centres of wealth and human might, is where true power lies.

> *We are also offered an alternative vision*

In my book I am trying to carry out a difficult balancing act. It isn't a commentary on Revelation, although the book does take the reader through the biblical text in some detail. It is not a devotional book, although to be absorbed into these images and visions is a spiritual experience of astonishing power. It is, I hope, a contemporary interpretation of a text that is absolutely intended to be reinterpreted in every generation. If that were not so, its use would have ended with the decline and fall of the Roman Empire, the 'Babylon' of Revelation, in the sixth century. In fact, though its relevance is timeless. We still have our Babylons and Babels and Romes. The four horsemen of war, plague, famine and conquest still ride through our 21st-century streets.

God and the Lamb are still on the throne, and the prayers of the saints still rise like incense, and the kingdoms of this world are become the kingdom of our Lord and of his Christ. This is no chronicle of despair but of hope.

This is no chronicle of despair

I have a feeling that this generation, familiar with the use of visual metaphor (think *Harry Potter*, *Dr Who*, *Lord of the Rings*), may be able to engage with the images of Revelation in a way that the immediately previous, more prosaic generations found difficult. This is no place for the literalist or the fact-finder, but for the one who can use imagination to open up understanding.

Facing the Darkness and Finding the Light could well be read as a Lent exercise or as a Sunday afternoon reflection, preferably with the biblical text open at the reader's side (although substantial passages are printed out in the book itself). But, as I have discovered in 'road-testing' it already, it also works very well for group study, because visions are visions and everyone sees a vision differently. Strictly speaking, there is no 'wrong' or 'right' way to interpret these fantastic images. Each one sees, and each one understands, which means that each one has an insight to share. Like walking through a picture gallery, we look and wonder and seek to understand—and it's much nicer to do that with some companions who are also looking, seeing and sharing.

The Greek name for Revelation is 'Apocalypse'. We live in apocalyptic times, at any rate judging by the number of films and television programmes with the word in their titles. This, however, is the true apocalypse, the unfolding not of a vision of the end of the world, but of the beginning of a new one.

To order a copy of Facing the Darkness and Finding the Light, *please turn to the order form on page 159.*

Working with children in the north-east

Chris Hudson

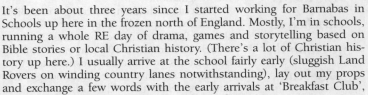

'Are you a king?' asked an awestruck child, seeing my plastic crown on a chair transformed into a 'throne' by a richly embroidered scarf. Not quite, mate.

It's been about three years since I started working for Barnabas in Schools up here in the frozen north of England. Mostly, I'm in schools, running a whole RE day of drama, games and storytelling based on Bible stories or local Christian history. (There's a lot of Christian history up here.) I usually arrive at the school fairly early (sluggish Land Rovers on winding country lanes notwithstanding), lay out my props and exchange a few words with the early arrivals at 'Breakfast Club', who are normally rather curious about this strange man setting things up on stage while they tuck into their toast and cereal. Then we have an assembly, where I set the theme for the day with a story, a song and a few questions and bad jokes…

After that, for hour after hour, groups of children troop in, to be regaled with moments of awe, wonder and a surprisingly large amount of silliness, all of it designed to stretch those mental muscles that wrestle with dilemmas such as 'Who am I?', 'Who is my neighbour?', or 'Who is this "God" person anyway?' The hardest classes are the youngest. They've only been in school for a few months at most, and are still learning the all-important skill of 'Sit still and look at me. I'm over here. I'm the one wearing the tie.' I do have some secret weapons—a guitar, props, and my collection of Beanie Babies. The guitar is a source of hypnotic fascination: it's in front of them, and it makes noises when I strum it. 'Are you a member of N-Dubz?' asked one boy, obviously a little confused.

The Beanie Babies are small stuffed toy animals: a bear, a tiger, a

> *Moments of awe, wonder and a surprisingly large amount of silliness*

cat, a monkey, a bird and some rats. After a song, I tell a story with the Beanie Babies, moving them around and asking questions about what they might be feeling at different points in the narrative. One story is about an argument in the playground (how might it have happened?); others centre on a stolen Easter egg (about saying sorry), a birthday present (saying thank you) or a version of the good Samaritan. They all try to get the children talking about feelings and asking 'What should happen next?' and they always relate to the day's theme. After exploring a few feelings and moral dilemmas, we move on to Bible stories told on the floor with Playmobil characters. This is really a child's version of Ignatian spiritual meditation—getting into the scene by using the imagination.

> *The diet is enriched as we climb the age-scale*

With older children, we can get into Bible stories more quickly. They have the social skills to follow instructions such as 'Stand in a circle as I count to 10', play more complicated games and discuss questions together. The diet is enriched as we climb the age-scale until we reach the oldest ones, who face tougher questions and requests for more detailed answers. The schools like it, and they tell us so. Teachers and head teachers tell each other as well, so bookings have risen hugely over the past year.

There are often some great comments when we talk about Bible stories. A question I like to ask is about how it might feel to be a sufferer of leprosy: and then to be touched by Jesus:

'Jesus turned him from a nobody into a somebody.'
'He could feel his heart melting as God touched him.'
'He would feel he was coming back to life.'

In another story, we act out the battle of Heavenfield, when Saint Oswald's tiny army prayed by a large wooden cross and then beat a larger pagan army to open up Northumbria to Christianity.

Afterwards, when asked if they had any questions or thoughts about the story, one lad walked over to the props table, took the king's crown, placed it decisively on the cross, and declared, *'That's what this story's saying.'*

Chris Hudson is a member of the Barnabas children's ministry team, based in the north-east of England.

Faith in the home: making Christmas different

Jane Butcher

Within BRF/Barnabas we have been giving specific time and input to developing the area of faith in the home. We recognise the need to support families in their spiritual development within their own homes and to work alongside church leaders as they seek to do the same.

For all families, we seek to offer practical ways to encourage, resource and support them to work out what being a Christian family means in the routines of everyday life. For church leaders, we seek to offer a wide range of appropriate articles and publications as well as offering support and practical ideas for the church's valuable role to encourage this area. (See www.faithinhomes.org.uk for further details.)

Many families who go to church see the value of integrating their faith into everyday family life but are not sure how to do it in a way that is relevant and interesting for their children. Equally, we hear from adults who are more than willing to explore faith in their homes but don't know where to start, particularly if they are one of the increasing numbers of people who haven't grown up with any background of faith or churchgoing.

> *Part of our vision is to encourage and resource these families*

Part of our vision is to encourage and resource these families as they begin or further their exciting journeys together. A natural way to do this is in celebrating Christian festivals in the home, and the upcoming season of Christmas is a perfect place to begin.

There seems to be an increasing feeling that Christmas is being 'taken over'. In fact, maybe it wouldn't be too extreme to suggest that

Christmas now seems to begin with 'S': shopping, stockings, satsumas, supermarkets, sprouts, Santa (believe in him or not!) and stress. However, for Christians the season means much more than this. It is about a gift—a gift given freely. That gift is, of course, the gift of Jesus—a Son and a Saviour.

Many of those other things have become part of our traditions, and this is not necessarily a bad thing. Tradition can bring some structure and routine, and may play an important part in our celebrations, but alongside the Christmas fairs, school productions, office parties and many other events, they can make us feel over-busy. It may seem that there is little time available to celebrate the faith aspect of the season, so maybe we should stop and refocus as individuals and as families.

Here are some suggestions to help us do this in a fun and faith-focused way.

> *Maybe we should stop and refocus as individuals and as families*

Make star-shaped cookies out of basic biscuit dough. While you sit down to enjoy them, read together the part of the Christmas story where the wise men follow the star to find Jesus (Matthew 2:1–11).

An alternative idea is to buy some small chocolate stars from the home baking section of the supermarket and place some on top of a Jaffa cake or chocolate digestive biscuit to represent the stars that shone in the dark night sky above the place where Jesus was born. You could add more effect by sprinkling edible gold glitter on the cakes or biscuits.

Make your own crib. Place a small box or cake baking case in the centre of a table. Fill it with some shredded paper, hay or straw (if available), or even some crushed-up shredded wheat. Imagine you are wise men. If you wanted to bring a precious gift to Jesus, what would you bring? Let each person answer in turn. If someone were giving you a precious gift, what would it be? A gift of happiness, peace, friendship or something else?

As a fun challenge, why not see how many words you can make from the word CHRISTMAS.

Make candle holders. Take a small plastic flowerpot holder, place a small piece of oasis on the centre and cover it with foil (to catch the melted candlewax). Stick in a small candle (a birthday cake candle, perhaps). Decorate the outside of the holder with leaves, holly, berries and so on. Light the candle at meal times to remember that Jesus came to be the light of the world.

You might also make a Christingle as a family:

- Take an orange and slice a small amount from the bottom so that it will stand on a plate or other flat surface. The orange represents the world.

- Fasten a piece of red tape or ribbon around the middle, using some sticky tape. The red ribbon represents the love or the blood of Christ.

- Lay a small square of silver foil on the top.

- Using a birthday cake candle and holder, push the holder firmly through the foil into the orange to hold the candle securely (the wax will drip on to the foil). The candle reminds us that Jesus is the light of the world.

- Load four cocktail sticks with raisins, sultanas, cherries or soft sweets, so that the points are covered. Insert them around the base of the candle. These represent the four seasons and the fruits of the earth—God's good gifts to us.

- Place the Christingles on a plate or flat surface. When you sit down to eat together, light the candles. Think of one thing that you would like to thank God for—for example, your home, friends, family, teachers, colleagues and so on.

However you choose to celebrate, enjoy this blessed season.

Jane Butcher is a member of the Barnabas children's ministry team, based in the Midlands. She is responsible for BRF's latest website: www.faithinhomes. org.uk. Jane is also the author of Messy Cooks, *a handbook for Messy Church catering teams (Barnabas, 2011), and* Bible Word Searches *(BRF, 2010). To order a copy of either of these books, please turn to the order form on page 159.*

Steve Brady

The Incredible
JOURNEY
Christmas from Genesis to Jesus

BRF ADVENT BOOK

An extract from
The Incredible Journey

The Bible presents the ultimate adventure—God's incredible, personal journey to the human race, which he loves with an amazing love, despite its repeated rejection of him. The story culminates in the coming of Jesus Christ, the incarnate God, in the events we celebrate every Christmas. In *The Incredible Journey*, BRF's Advent book for 2011, author Steve Brady shows how Jesus has come to take us home to God, no matter what our starting point. The following extract is the reading for 21 December.

Nehemiah: a builder

In the month of Kislev in the twentieth year, while I was in the citadel of Susa, Hanani, one of my brothers, came from Judah with some other men, and I questioned them about the Jewish remnant that survived the exile, and also about Jerusalem. They said to me, 'Those who survived the exile and are back in the province are in great trouble and disgrace. The wall of Jerusalem is broken down, and its gates have been burned with fire.' When I heard these things, I sat down and wept. For some days I mourned and fasted and prayed before the God of heaven. Then I said: 'O Lord, God of heaven, the great and awesome God, who keeps his covenant of love with those who love him and obey his commands, let your ear be attentive and your eyes open to hear the prayer your servant is praying before you day and night for your servants, the people of Israel... We have acted very wickedly towards you. We have not obeyed the commands, decrees and laws you gave your servant Moses. Remember the instruction you gave your servant Moses, saying, "If you are unfaithful, I will scatter you among the nations, but if you return to me and obey my commands, then even if your exiled people are at the farthest horizon, I will gather them from there and bring them to the place I have chosen as a dwelling for my Name." ... O Lord, let your ear be attentive to the prayer of this your servant and to the prayer of your servants who delight in revering your name. Give your servant success today by granting him favour in the presence of this man.' I was cupbearer to the king.

NEHEMIAH 1:1–11

To say that Nehemiah is not a name we usually associate with the Christmas story is more than a mild understatement. For many of us, even finding the location of his book is, I suspect, an accomplishment! But I believe he qualifies for a Lifetime Achievement Award for his often overlooked contribution to the establishment of the kingdom of God and his key part in *The Incredible Journey*. Really? Wasn't he just a builder, after all is said and done?

Nehemiah lived at a critical period in Israel's history, the fifth century bc. Although now back in their own land, and with a rebuilt temple, all was not well with the Jewish nation. Jerusalem, 'the joy of the whole earth' according to Psalm 48:2, was anything but. Rather, its wall was 'broken down, and its gates… burned with fire'. When the news reached him in 445bc, while he was living some 800 miles away in one of the Persian capitals, Susa, it sent Nehemiah into a tailspin of fasting, mourning and prayer. Why such angst over a semi-derelict city? One reason was that without a properly constituted and protected city, complete with gates and walls, Jewish identity would be threatened and maybe lost in a hostile world.

Why such angst over a semi-derelict city?

The last chapter of Nehemiah illustrates the point vividly: it records the previous neglect and abuse of the temple, desecration of the sabbath, mixed marriages and more.

Why did those things matter? The answer lies in a statement of Jesus centuries later, while he was talking to a Samaritan woman: 'Salvation is from the Jews' (John 4:22). This had been part of God's overarching purpose from the day he called Abram to follow him and become the father of a nation through which he intended to bless the world (Genesis 12:1–3). That divine plan, the outworking of which had been underway for centuries, was once again threatened in Nehemiah's time. God's intention was to come to this world personally in Jesus Christ, and through the vehicle of the Jewish people. If that nation became intermingled with other nations and lost, then the bottom line may be starkly expressed: 'No Jews, no Jesus'. 'No Jesus' would mean an aborted rescue mission to the human race.

I'm not suggesting, of course, that Nehemiah had all this figured out in detail. Like the prophets, as the apostle Peter expressed it, he too was 'trying to find out the time and circumstances' concerning the 'sufferings and glories' of Christ (see 1 Peter 1:11–12). But he persisted by serving his own contemporary situation and future generations too.

The first six chapters of the book are stirring stuff. In the first chapter, we meet Nehemiah the worshipper, enjoying intimacy with God—the necessary foundation for any usefulness in God's kingdom. Providentially, as 'cupbearer to the king', he was in an ideal position to influence royal policy. In turn, that influence rewarded him with a governorship in Judah and the role of workman, as the next two chapters illustrate. Faith, courage, vision, tenacity, teamwork and sacrifice are all involved in any great scheme for God. Nehemiah was the type of leader who led from the front. Others recognised his leadership and joined in the great building project. Chapters 4—6 introduce Nehemiah the warrior. God's work is always opposed. Sometimes, it is threatened by outside forces such as Sanballat and his henchmen (Nehemiah 4:7). At other times, there are problems within the camp, as inconsistencies surface within the believing community and abuses have to be dealt with, as in Nehemiah 5. Finally, in the midst of everything else, a leader may often come under sustained scrutiny and personal attack, as chapter 6 makes painfully clear.

Are you involved in some work for God? Is it tough? Are you discouraged or tempted to give up? The truth is that many of us often do not see how our small part fits into the 'big picture' of God's ways, but that should not deter us from faithfully doing what is before us day by day. Local churches and projects for the Lord 'grow and build themselves up in love, as each part does its work' (see Ephesians 4:16).

So then, Nehemiah was 'only a builder', yet he passed a lasting legacy on to future generations—Jerusalem, the city of God. To that city, one day, another builder came. Like Nehemiah, he too wept for it (Luke 19:41). Then he did what no one else could do: he suffered 'outside the city gate to make... people holy' and set them on a journey to a 'city that is to come' (Hebrews 13:12, 14). It's called 'the new Jerusalem' (Revelation 21:2). It is Christ's eternal legacy to his people.

Reflection

I am only one,
But still I am one.
I cannot do everything,
But still I can do something;
And because I cannot do everything,
I will not refuse to do the something that I can do.

EDWARD EVERETT HALE (1822–1909)

To order a copy of this book, please use the order form on page 159.

SUPPORTING BRF'S MINISTRY

As a Christian charity, BRF is involved in five distinct yet complementary areas.

- **BRF** (www.brf.org.uk) resources adults for their spiritual journey through Bible reading notes, books, and a programme of quiet days and teaching days. BRF also provides the infrastructure that supports our other four specialist ministries.
- **Foundations21** (www.foundations21.org.uk) provides flexible and innovative ways for individuals and groups to explore their Christian faith and discipleship through a multimedia internet-based resource.
- **Messy Church** (www.messychurch.org.uk), led by Lucy Moore, enables churches all over the UK (and increasingly abroad) to reach children and adults beyond the fringes of the church .
- **Barnabas in Churches** (www.barnabasinchurches.org.uk) helps churches to support, resource and develop their children's ministry with the under-11s more effectively .
- **Barnabas in Schools** (www.barnabasinschools.org.uk) enables primary school children and teachers to explore Christianity creatively and bring the Bible alive within RE and Collective Worship.

At the heart of BRF's ministry is a desire to equip adults and children for Christian living—helping them to read and understand the Bible, to explore prayer and to grow as disciples of Jesus. We need your help to make a real impact on the local church, local schools and the wider community.

- You could support BRF's ministry with a donation or standing order (using the response form overleaf).
- You could consider making a bequest to BRF in your will.
- You could encourage your church to support BRF as part of your church's giving to home mission—perhaps focusing on a specific area of our ministry, or a particular member of our Barnabas team.
- Most important of all, you could support BRF with your prayers.

If you would like to discuss how a specific gift or bequest could be used in the development of our ministry, please phone 01865 319700 or email enquiries@brf.org.uk.

Whatever you can do or give, we thank you for your support.

BRF MINISTRY APPEAL RESPONSE FORM

Name _____

Address _____

_____ Postcode _____

Telephone _____ Email _____

Gift Aid Declaration

❏ I am a UK taxpayer. I want BRF to treat as Gift Aid Donations all donations I make from 6 April 2000 until I notify you otherwise.

Signature _____ Date _____

❏ I would like to support BRF's ministry with a regular donation by standing order

Standing Order – Banker's Order

To the Manager, Name of Bank/Building Society

Address _____

_____ Postcode _____

Sort Code _____ Account Name _____

Account No _____

Please pay Royal Bank of Scotland plc, Drummonds, 49 Charing Cross,
London SW1A 2DX (Sort Code 16-00-38), for the account of BRF A/C No. 00774151

The sum of _____ pounds on ___ /___ /___ (insert date) and thereafter the same amount on the same day of each month annually until further notice.

Signature _____ Date _____

Single donation

❏ I enclose my cheque/credit card/Switch card details for a donation of
£5 £10 £25 £50 £100 £250 (other) £ _____ to support BRF's ministry

Card no. [ ][ ][ ][ ][ ][ ][ ][ ][ ][ ][ ][ ][ ][ ][ ][ ]

Expires [ ][ ][ ][ ]   Security code [ ][ ][ ]   Issue no. [ ][ ][ ]

Signature _____ Date _____

Please use my donation for ❏ BRF ❏ Foundations21 ❏ Messy Church
❏ Barnabas in Churches ❏ Barnabas in Schools

❏ Please send me information about making a bequest to BRF in my will.

Please detach and send this completed form to: Richard Fisher, BRF,
15 The Chambers, Vineyard, Abingdon OX14 3FE. BRF is a Registered Charity (No.233280)

 GL 0311

❏ I would like to take out a subscription myself:

Your name _____

Your address _____

_____ Postcode _____

Tel _____ Email _____

Please send *Guidelines* beginning with the January 2012 / May 2012 / September 2012 issue: (delete as applicable)

(please tick box)	UK	SURFACE	AIR MAIL
GUIDELINES	❏ £14.70	❏ £16.50	❏ £19.95
GUIDELINES 3-year sub	❏ £36.90		
GUIDELINES pdf download	❏ £11.70 (UK and overseas)		

❏ I would like to give a gift subscription (please complete both name and address sections above and below):

Gift subscription name _____

Gift subscription address _____

_____ Postcode _____

Gift message (20 words max. or include your own gift card for the recipient)

_____

_____

Please send *Guidelines* beginning with the January 2012 / May 2012 / September 2012 issue: (delete as applicable)

(please tick box)	UK	SURFACE	AIR MAIL
GUIDELINES	❏ £14.70	❏ £16.50	❏ £19.95
GUIDELINES 3-year sub	❏ £36.90		
GUIDELINES pdf download	❏ £11.70 (UK and overseas)		

Please complete your payment details overleaf.

To set up a direct debit, please also complete the form on page 157 and send it to BRF with this form.

SUBSCRIPTION PAYMENT DETAILS

Please complete the payment details below and send with appropriate payment and completed Subscriptions order form to:

BRF, 15 The Chambers, Vineyard, Abingdon OX14 3FE

Total enclosed £ _____ (cheques should be made payable to 'BRF')

Please charge my Visa ❑ Mastercard ❑ Switch card ❑ with £

Card no: | | | | | | | | | | | | | | | | | | | |

Expires | | | | Security code | | |

Issue no (Switch only) | | | |

Signature (essential if paying by card) _____

Direct Debit

Now you can pay for your annual subscription to BRF notes using Direct Debit. You need only give your bank details once, and the payment is made automatically every year until you cancel it.

If you would like to pay by Direct Debit, please use the form opposite. Please fill in your bank's name and address, and your sort code and account number. You must also fill in your BRF account number, which can be found in the top left hand corner of your renewal reminders.

You are fully covered by the Direct Debit Guarantee:

The Direct Debit Guarantee

- This Guarantee is offered by all Banks and Building Societies that take part in the Direct Debit Scheme. The efficiency and security of the Scheme is monitored and protected by your own Bank or Building Society.
- If the amounts to be paid or the payment dates change, BRF will notify you 14 days in advance of your account being debited or as otherwise agreed.
- If an error is made by BRF or your Bank or Building Society, you are guaranteed a full and immediate refund from your branch of the amount paid.
- You can cancel a Direct Debit any time by writing to your Bank or Building Society. Please also send a copy of your letter to us.

❑ Please do not send me further information about BRF publications.

BRF is a Registered Charity

INSTRUCTION TO YOUR BANK/BUILDING SOCIETY TO PAY DIRECT DEBITS

DIRECT Debit

Service User Number: | 5 | 5 | 8 | 2 | 2 | 9 |

1. Full postal address of your branch

To: The Manager _____

_____ Bank/Bldg. Soc.

Address_____

_____ Postcode _____

2. Name(s) of account holder

3. Bank/Building Society account no

4. Branch sort code

Banks/Building Societies may refuse to accept instructions to pay direct debits from some types of account.

5. Instruction to your Bank/Building Society

Please pay BRF Direct Debits from the account detailed on this instruction, subject to the safeguards assured by the Direct Debit Guarantee.

Signatures of Account Holders

Signature(s) _____

Address _____

_____

Date _____

QUIET SPACES ORDER FORM

Quiet Spaces is published three times a year, in May, September and January. To take out a subscription, please complete this form, indicating the month in which you would like your subscription to begin.

❑ I would like to take out a subscription myself:

Your name _____

Your address _____

_____ Postcode _____

Tel _____ Email _____

❑ I would like to give a gift subscription (please complete both name and address sections above and below):

Gift subscription name _____

Gift subscription address _____

_____ Postcode _____

Gift message (20 words max. or include your own gift card for the recipient)

_____

_____

Please send beginning with the January 2012 / May 2012 / September 2012 issue: (delete as applicable)

	UK	SURFACE	AIR MAIL
(please tick box)			
QUIET SPACES	❑ £16.95	❑ £18.45	❑ £20.85

Please complete the payment details below and send with appropriate payment to: **BRF, 15 The Chambers, Vineyard, Abingdon OX14 3FE**

Total enclosed £ _____ (cheques should be made payable to 'BRF')

Please charge my Visa ❑ Mastercard ❑ Switch card ❑ with £ _____

Card no: ⬚⬚⬚⬚ ⬚⬚⬚⬚ ⬚⬚⬚⬚ ⬚⬚⬚⬚ ⬚⬚

Expires ⬚⬚⬚⬚ Security code ⬚⬚⬚

Issue no (Switch only) ⬚⬚⬚⬚

Signature (essential if paying by card) _____

GL 0311

BRF PUBLICATIONS ORDER FORM

Please ensure that you complete and send off both sides of this order form.
Please send me the following book(s):

		Quantity	Price	Total
003 5	The Incredible Journey (S. Brady)	_____	£6.99	_____
709 9	Pilgrims to the Manger (N. Starkey)	_____	£7.99	_____
835 5	Facing the Darkness and Finding the Light (D. Winter)	_____	£6.99	_____
814 0	Messy Cooks (J. Butcher)	_____	£5.99	_____
789 1	Bible Word Searches (J. Butcher)	_____	£6.99	_____
856 0	Creative Ideas for Advent and Christmas (J. Tibbs)	_____	£7.99	_____
024 0	The Baby Born at Christmas (S.A. Wright)	_____	£6.99	_____
025 7	My Storytime Bible (R. Boyle)	_____	£9.99	_____

Total cost of books £ _____

Donation £ _____

Postage and packing £ _____

TOTAL £ _____

POSTAGE AND PACKING CHARGES				
order value	UK	Europe	Surface	Air Mail
£7.00 & under	£1.25	£3.00	£3.50	£5.50
£7.01–£30.00	£2.25	£5.50	£6.50	£10.00
Over £30.00	free	prices on request		

For more information about new books and special offers, visit www.brfonline.org.uk.

See over for payment details.

All prices are correct at time of going to press, are subject to the prevailing rate of VAT and may be subject to change without prior warning.

PAYMENT DETAILS

WAYS TO ORDER BRF RESOURCES

Christian bookshops: All good Christian bookshops stock BRF publications. For your nearest stockist, please contact BRF.

Telephone: The BRF office is open between 09.15 and 17.30.
To place your order, phone 01865 319700; fax 01865 319701.

Web: Visit www.brfonline.org.uk

By post: Please complete the payment details below and send with appropriate payment and completed order form to:

BRF, 15 The Chambers, Vineyard, Abingdon OX14 3FE

Name _____

Address _____

_____ Postcode _____

Telephone _____

Email _____

Total enclosed £ _____ (cheques should be made payable to 'BRF')

Please charge my Visa ❏ Mastercard ❏ Switch card ❏ with £ _____

Card no: [ ][ ][ ][ ][ ][ ][ ][ ][ ][ ][ ][ ][ ][ ][ ][ ][ ][ ]

Expires [ ][ ][ ][ ]   Security code [ ][ ][ ]

Issue no (Switch only) [ ][ ][ ][ ]

Signature (essential if paying by credit/Switch) _____

❏ Please do not send me further information about BRF publications.

BRF is a Registered Charity